Crash Course

ISBN: 1484848659
ISBN-13: 9781484848654

Library of Congress Control Number: 2013910301
CreateSpace Independent Publishing Platform,
North Charleston, South Carolina

Crash Course

A Head of School, His Son's Addiction,
and Lessons For Schools and Families

***

Michael D. Pratt, Ph.D.

Contents

Acknowledgements

As I initially contemplated writing this book, I knew I needed my son David's permission. Central to the story is his descent into alcoholism and addiction and his eventual recovery, so it was essential that he be willing to have his disease—and the difficulties that came as a result of it—publicly exposed. He not only agreed, he encouraged me in my efforts and cooperated by revealing things I hadn't known before. I am grateful for his courage.

David's use came to light during his junior year at Brentwood School, where I was the Head of School. What in other circumstances would have been simply a personal matter was, in this case, the most difficult challenge in my career. Without the wise counsel and steadfast support of my Board Chair, Richard Sandler, I could not have continued to lead the school successfully.

Numerous counselors and other professionals in the recovery community were lifelines for David. Three deserve special mention: Jim Earnhardt was David's personal counselor in Los Angeles; Betty Wyman advised me and my wife Susan about the best resources for David; and Richard Rogg took David in twice at Promises. Without their compassion and generosity, I doubt that David would have recovered.

Even though I am solely responsible for any flaws that remain in this book, I am grateful to friends and family who read it and provided their feedback and encouragement. Chief among them is my good friend and equally good editor, Marian Cavanagh.

Michael D. Pratt

In the many moments when I despaired, doubting that David would make it or that I could continue to lead my school effectively, Susan provided the strength and support I needed. This book, and the good that I hope it will do, would not be possible without her steadfastness, love, and devotion.

Foreword

My name is David, and I am an alcoholic. I wish I could point to a specific time when it all started; but the fact is, I don't know. I've always liked to feel different; anything is better than what I'm feeling at any given moment. I could throw out such clichés as, "I wasn't comfortable in my own skin"; "I didn't want to feel" … the list goes on. They're probably all true, but I've never been able to point to one thing that caused me to behave as I have.

I was born in Alexandria, Virginia, to a loving family, and was given all I needed to be successful. There is no one thing I can point to that led me to drugs and alcohol. I smoked my first cigarette with a neighborhood friend when I was about ten years old, and I remember being light-headed—a new and exciting sensation. From that point on, I took every opportunity to chase that feeling, trying to find something that made me feel even better. When I was around fourteen, I found it: alcohol. I had heard stories from my friends about drinking. One night when my parents were out, I decided to explore their liquor cabinet. I probably had three or four drinks, and then lay on the floor of my bedroom, amazed by how good I felt. I didn't see any problem with my behavior. Every so often, when I had the opportunity, I would have a few drinks; but that was it. It wasn't until my family moved to Los Angeles so that my dad could become Brentwood's Head of School that a new classmate introduced me to drugs. From that point on, getting high consumed my thoughts.

Once that became my most important goal, trouble inevitably followed. Even though I got busted for using drugs and was suspended from school, I didn't think I had a problem and didn't think my behavior had anything to do with anybody else. I wasn't worried that drugs might harm me, and it didn't occur to me that my actions could jeopardize my dad's credibility as Head of School.

My use of alcohol and drugs would ultimately send me to a string of rehabs and cost me countless opportunities; but like so many alcoholics and addicts, I was in denial. It was only when I hit bottom and made my own decision to go to rehab that I got sober. It was the only opportunity I'd taken advantage of for a very long time.

I went to Promises twice, and the second time I found success. I embraced Alcoholics Anonymous, and I have been able to stay sober for more than five years. It hasn't been an easy road; in fact, things got much more complicated. I'm now married and have a stepson and twin boys. They're all special needs children; but I see those challenges as a blessing. I have three beautiful children and a life I wouldn't trade for the world. Despite the difficulties, I've been given the tools, through sobriety, to face any situation. I work in the Operations Department at Promises, where I have gained many good skills. My work also keeps me attached to the program at all times. I live my life one day at a time; that's a common cliché, but one that certainly applies to every facet of my life. My name is David; I'm an alcoholic, and this is my story.

Introduction

The pages that follow in many respects tell a common story: an individual's struggle with addiction and its impact on the addict's family. Countless books have been written on this subject. Some have happy endings, some don't, but all describe the addict's downward spiral and the stress this descent puts on the family and other loved ones.

This story follows a similar pattern, except that my journey was both personal and professional. In my first year as the Head of School at Brentwood School in Los Angeles, my first drug case involved my son, David. In addition to the personal crisis that any father goes through when finding out that his child is experimenting with drugs and faces school discipline, this situation represented an enormous professional challenge. I was responsible for protecting the integrity of the school while simultaneously supporting my son.

My wife, Susan Key, and I would learn over time that our son's use had moved well beyond typical adolescent experimentation. In the process of discovering a lot about the disease of alcoholism and addiction, I came to understand why so many adolescents use, and the resulting devastating consequences to their health and education, as well as to their families, friends, and communities. I dedicated myself to creating approaches to mitigating adolescent alcohol and drug use and to supporting those students who ran off the rails.

Far too many schools either deny there's a problem or respond in a draconian way: expulsion of the offending student. Neither approach is effective. I believe it's vital for schools to understand the reasons for and extent of

Michael D. Pratt

adolescent experimentation and to respond in a humane way that engages the entire school community, protects the school's integrity, supports the individual offender, and develops a school culture based on trust and openness.

In describing my son's struggles and my work at Brentwood School, I hope to help other parents and schools successfully navigate a national crisis in adolescent well-being.

Busted

David only dropped by my office to ask for money; since that kind of request wouldn't require a chaperone, I was immediately concerned when he showed up accompanied by his English teacher. He'd taken his English semester exam earlier in the day, so I suspected that the unplanned meeting meant something had gone very badly. His teacher said that David had something he needed to tell me. Between her ominous tone and my son's ashen pallor, I knew the news couldn't be good; but I had no notion just how bad it would be, or how deeply and irrevocably it would impact our family.

"I ate some mushrooms and couldn't finish my exam." With my mind racing in utter confusion, I think I managed, "you what?" I got slightly more detail when he mumbled that he'd gone off campus between exams, eaten some hallucinogenic mushrooms, and couldn't focus sufficiently to complete his exam essay. When I asked why he'd done this, he said he thought the experience might give him some ideas. He didn't seem interested in my suggestion that studying might have been a better option. I told him to go home and that we'd talk more that evening. One semester was not yet complete, and I had my first drug case as the new Head of School: my son.

Susan and I had seen a couple of small signs earlier in the school year; but, as do many parents, we'd largely dismissed the warnings. We'd moved to Los Angeles in the summer of 2001 for my new position at Brentwood School, a prestigious college prep school in one of the most affluent areas in the country. I had previously served as Academic

Michael D. Pratt

Dean at Menlo School in Northern California, where our son had been a student from sixth through tenth grades. We were all quite happy there; but I had gotten the itch to be a head of school and, after an extensive search, was appointed to my new position. We anticipated that the move might be difficult for David because he'd be leaving many close friends and would have to make new ones. He'd also have to figure out a new school culture and study with new teachers, all under the microscope of being the Head's son. I had seen difficulties surrounding these transitions many times, so I was relieved when he decided to join the school's football team and initially performed well in his classes.

But then the little warning signals began. One evening he announced he wanted to quit the team, because he wasn't getting much playing time and wasn't enjoying the experience. I reminded him that he'd never played organized football before, so there was, of course, a steep learning curve, and that he'd inevitably earn more playing time as he got more familiar with the game. Though he protested that it was no fun, I insisted he complete the season and agreed he wouldn't have to play in his senior year if he didn't want to. I was disappointed, but I understood.

A few days after this conversation, the Dean of Students dropped by my office to tell me that a girl had reported seeing David with a baggie of marijuana at school. The Dean explained that she couldn't confirm the report and that it could be a mistake, or nothing more than a rumor. When I asked David about it on our way home, he was strongly defensive, categorically denied it, and said he hated Brentwood School because everybody was in everybody else's business, and rumors ran like wildfire.

Susan and I talked it over and agreed to pay close attention to David's affect and behavior, but we actually didn't believe the report had any validity. Our views about drug use were clear; we were convinced he had good friends and wouldn't engage in such risky behavior. We didn't dismiss

2

this warning, but neither did we look objectively at what was beginning to be a pattern.

Soon afterward, Susan was doing the laundry and discovered a pack of cigarettes in a pair of his pants. Even though taking a smoke might not be a matter of great concern in the larger context of adolescent experimentation, we were alarmed and decided to confront him. In the face of this tangible evidence, he confessed that he'd started to smoke just after we'd moved to Los Angeles. We made clear that we wouldn't tolerate his smoking and were prepared to cut off his allowance to ensure that he couldn't purchase cigarettes. We also determined that he should start seeing a therapist; we believed his behavior might point to some underlying psychological issues that should be examined.

Why such a strong reaction to smoking? We knew that David had only recently begun to smoke, and even though we suspected he did so more than he admitted, we felt the early discovery made it possible to end the habit before it posed long-term health risks. More importantly, we viewed it as a serious breach of trust. We were not unusually naïve parents, but we were unnerved by his secret life in an area in which we held extremely strong views.

Susan and I met with David's therapist first. We were concerned that he might see our alarm as an overreaction; to our surprise, he gently suggested it was likely that our son was experimenting with more than tobacco. Even though we'd had the other warnings, we expressed our doubt. After David's therapy session, we felt good that we were responding proactively and had taken an important step to resolve whatever issues were troubling him. So on the afternoon that he confessed to having eaten mushrooms, I understood how hopelessly naïve I'd been. I didn't realize, however, that my education was just beginning.

Past

Most problems come unbidden, but substance abuse is a problem that most Heads of secondary schools eventually must face. Mine, however, was unusually complicated. The landscape was a minefield—especially so in this high-pressure culture.

The year began with the challenges and heartbreak of the 9/11 attacks; but, as in so many other difficult situations, the school community became even closer. We moved through that time together, and the result was a remarkably smooth and positive first six months in my new position. That is, until I found myself facing a different challenge—one that would test both my leadership and character. In some respects, I was well prepared; in others, I was in uncharted territory. I had worked for many years in independent schools and was very clear about my own values. But I was new to being a Head of School, and new to Brentwood School and West Los Angeles—the latter two could hardly have been further from my personal experience.

Born in 1953, I grew up in Martinsville, Virginia, a small town a bit east of the Blue Ridge Mountains. At the time, it was a thriving manufacturing center for furniture and textiles. For a period, the town boasted that it was the "sweatshirt capital of the world." Perhaps not the most elegant title, but the factories ensured employment for everyone willing and able to work. It was also an important auction center for tobacco. Both industries have now all but disappeared; furniture and textile manufacturing have been moved abroad, and tobacco farming is no longer profitable. Today it has one of the highest unemployment rates in the state, with an even smaller population than when I lived there.

My father was a fireman—a respectable blue-collar job; my mother, who had become pregnant shortly after they married, stayed home to raise a family that grew quickly. I was the third of four children born in a seven-year period, and my family had to make do on the one working-class salary. There were no frills; we never took a vacation, unless you count an occasional trip to my grandparents' fruit farm, where my father would help with a harvest. My older brother and sister were able to take piano lessons from the choir director at our church, but when it might have been my turn, there was no money. We ate enough (always at home), were adequately clothed (lots of hand-me-downs), and had a roof over our heads, even though that roof covered a small house. We attended the town's public school.

When I was 12, my father suffered a serious heart attack and was immediately hospitalized. In less than a month, still in the hospital, he had another, this one fatal. Just days earlier, my mother found out she was pregnant with her fifth child. In order to avoid a potential setback in my father's recovery, the doctor had urged her to delay giving him this news, so he died before she was able to tell him. In addition to our devastating loss, what had been a narrow means of existence was now considerably tighter.

Education was not an important value in my family. No member on either side had ever attended college. My father was a high school dropout and my mother was one of 16 graduates from a little mountain school. After completing high school, she moved to Martinsville to take a job and, in fairly short order, met my father, married, and settled into family life. With a growing brood, it's not surprising that there was little emphasis on study in our house.

Until my junior year in high school, I had little interest in academics. Music and sports were the only activities that kept me engaged and prevented me from dropping out, as my father had done. Without the intervention of my eleventh grade English teacher, Pat Heberer, I would likely have followed in my parents' and older siblings' footsteps: no college, get married, start a family. I had done nothing to distinguish myself in school, so I thought I'd as likely go to Mars as to college. Yet for reasons that still remain unclear to me, Mrs. Heberer saw potential I didn't know I had; she helped me to develop a love of learning and insisted that I go to college. First at Virginia Commonwealth University and then at the University of Virginia, a whole new world opened up to me.

In college, a childhood love of stories about the past blossomed into an abiding passion for history. I was particularly drawn to nineteenth and twentieth-century European History. As I began to have a professional interest in the subject, I came to understand that it was important to know the languages of the cultures I was studying. I took up German, French, and Italian so I could read primary sources. By my senior year, I knew I wanted to be a professional historian, so I applied to several leading graduate programs and took my master's and doctorate degrees in Modern European Intellectual History from Harvard University. I still recall with wonder phoning my mother to tell her I had been admitted to Harvard. Her response: "What's that?" When you've grown up in the Blue Ridge Mountains and raised a family in a little town in Virginia, it's possible never to have heard of Harvard.

My aim was to be a college history professor, even though I understood that the market for professors in all the liberal arts fields was terribly depressed. At a reception for the newly admitted history graduate students, the History Department Chair unceremoniously told us that fewer than half of our group would complete our degrees, and only a fraction of that number would find teaching positions in universities. He was right.

I was undaunted, however, by such grim prospects. In part, I believed that I would be among the lucky minority who would finish my advanced degrees and land a desirable position. Despite a childhood that was at times uncertain and insecure, I just always believed that things would turn out well. I was also thrilled to be able to study at such a place as Harvard. I was lucky to have received a generous financial aid package in addition to a stipend, so I was being paid to study history. Job, no job; I was happy to do what I loved and let the future take care of itself.

While there, I worked with uncompromising dedication. In my eagerness to complete my master's and doctorate as quickly as possible, I passed up opportunities for research abroad that no doubt would have deepened my knowledge and understanding. My sense of urgency was in part pathological: I identified very closely with my father, who had died at thirty-eight; and I thought it unlikely that I would live any longer than that. Instead, I conducted my research mostly at Harvard and the Library of Congress. I completed my degrees in five-and-a-half years—warp speed for a history Ph.D. in the early 1980s.

Having finished my doctoral work in the summer of 1981, I awaited position announcements and planned to enter the job market in the early winter with my degree in hand. In the meantime, I needed to earn some money; so I sent my resume to a teacher placement service, hoping to be a substitute teacher until I landed a university job. Just as schools were opening in the fall of 1981, I got a call from St. Agnes School, an excellent Episcopal girls' school in Alexandria, Virginia, to interview for a full-time substitute teaching position. I met with the Director of the upper school, who offered me the job. I inherited the classes of a legendary History Department Chairperson who, finding out she was terminally ill, had just taken her own life. These were inauspicious circumstances in which to come into a school, but I was determined to do my best to contribute and to make the most of what I planned to be a short-term commitment. Little did I know that I had accepted a position that would determine the course of my professional life.

It took me very little time to fall in love with my work. Having attended a public school myself, I knew almost nothing about private schools generally or independent schools in particular. I was delighted to discover that my students were bright and eager to learn. Their parents were supportive and respectful of the school's administrators and teachers. My colleagues were exceptionally talented and committed to bringing out the best in their students. Even the extra duties that independent school teachers are expected to perform were interesting to me. Well, I didn't particularly enjoy chaperoning dances: too much loud, bad music. But I coached two sports, was the faculty sponsor for the student newspaper, and was moderator for the school's Model United Nations team. I loved being engaged in the life of the school in a way that college professors are not. I knew from my own high school experience that sports, the arts, and co-curricular activities are places where students make vital connections to their school.

After a couple of months, I made an appointment with the upper school Director to let her know how much I was enjoying my work. I was pleased to be told that she was happy with the job I was doing, and she asked me if I had given any thought to remaining at the school. I agreed to stay for the entire year, but then signed a contract for the following one. I was hooked, and ultimately stayed from 1981 to 1993. During my tenure at St. Agnes (subsequently St. Stephen's and St. Agnes after the schools merged in 1991), I came to understand that the culture of independent schools is radically different from the public schools of my own experience. They are able to devote a level of attention to every student in a way that's not possible in public schools. I will always be grateful that my first job was at St. Agnes and that I was able to develop my teaching skills with the support of so many outstanding colleagues.

Michael D. Pratt

While at St. Agnes, I also began teaching as an adjunct history professor at Marymount University in Arlington, Virginia. In 1993, I was invited to work for a year as a program officer in the Division of Education Programs at the National Endowment for the Humanities, where I remained for just over two years. During that time, I was again privileged to work with exceptionally bright colleagues. I gained administrative experience, learned about academic trends at both the collegiate and pre-collegiate levels, and worked on the Endowment's first "teaching with technology" initiative. My tenure ended with the 1994 congressional election that resulted in Republicans taking control of the House of Representatives. The new majority hoped to abolish the Endowments for both the Arts and the Humanities. The first step was a severe budget cutback that forced the Endowments to conduct major staffing reductions. As a recent arrival, I knew I would be on the list. Even though I didn't relish the uncertainty that came from this turn of events, I was very eager to return to an independent school in a leadership role.

Ready for an adventure, I accepted a position as Academic Dean at Menlo School, an outstanding independent school in Northern California, where I remained for five years. I couldn't have asked for better mentoring than I got from Norm Colb, the Head of School, who was extremely generous in his counsel and involved me in a wider scope of issues than would typically be the case for an Academic Dean. Even so, I was not routinely involved with student discipline, except in those cases that were breaches of academic ethics. In my time there, I recall only two cases related to alcohol or drugs; in those instances, my opinion was sought, but I didn't participate in the deliberations or have responsibility for the final decision. Nothing, in fact, had prepared me to deal with a case as complex as the one I now faced.

Zero

When I found out about David's behavior, it was immediately clear that he must go before the school's Honor Board, since being under the influence of alcohol or drugs while on campus or at a school-sponsored event was a violation of policy. At the time, Brentwood School's Dean of Students was responsible for convening this Board, which weighed evidence, considered the circumstances of the case, and made recommendations to the Head of School, who was ultimately responsible for all disciplinary decisions. I knew that this case involved an obvious conflict of interest for me. A Head of School's decisions must be objective, fair, and clearly perceived to be independent. Since this was a case that could end in my son's expulsion, I knew I couldn't possibly meet those standards, and that I needed to recuse myself from the proceedings.

The spotlight couldn't have been brighter. It was my first disciplinary case, I was the new Head of School, and it involved my son and drug use. There had been a minor cheating incident within a month of my arrival; but since it happened during summer school, there was no Honor Board, and the case was easily and quickly resolved. David's case was entirely different. No matter where it occurred, this situation involved my son and would have been difficult, but the high-pressure atmosphere and celebrity-culture scrutiny that comes into play at Brentwood made matters even more difficult. I understood that my response to the crisis carried tremendous symbolic weight.

I was already on record with my views about student alcohol and drug use. During my interview at Brentwood,

Michael D. Pratt

a member of the upper school faculty had asked my opinions on appropriate consequences for a student who broke their alcohol and drug policy. I didn't know their specific policy details at the time; but, of course, no school supports illicit use. I responded that schools necessarily took student alcohol and drug use seriously and that, for the student's and the school community's sake, there must be consequences. That said, I believed in resorting to expulsion only in the most extreme circumstances: the student had offended before or was dealing drugs to other students. My reasoning was that a student who is an occasional user and not a dealer does not represent a threat to other students and could be dissuaded from further use or treated if an addiction had developed, and that retaining the student in school gave a chance to affect behavior—an opportunity that was lost with expulsion. So I was clear in my response: there must be a consequence, but only in extreme cases would I opt for expulsion. I didn't know how the faculty took my response, but I was on record.

I also didn't know that, near the end of my predecessor's tenure, a drug use case had rocked the school. A group of juniors participating in the school's annual East Coast college trip had been discovered smoking marijuana. When they were not expelled, many people in the school community wondered why, and believed the Head of School had changed policy and become less vigilant in dealing with student drug use. I don't know all the facts, and won't speculate on the way the case was handled, but I later understood that the perception of laxity was the context for the interview question. My response at the time was an honest one, but given without being aware of the context and the tensions within the community about this issue.

Later I discovered that many thought my views were overly permissive. In fact, I don't and never have held *laissez-faire* views on alcohol or drug use. Perhaps rare for someone who came of age during the sixties, I was a teetotaler: when I was in high school, I never took so much as a sip

12

of beer or a puff of a cigarette. My abstinence was not the product of supposed moral superiority, religious conviction, or a killjoy disposition. I remained on the straight and narrow out of fear.

As a child, far too many social occasions ended with my mother drunk and my father remote and silent. My family did not party a lot—our finances didn't make that possible—but we would occasionally attend Fire Department picnics where my mother drank heavily. The same thing happened at most Christmas and Thanksgiving dinners. Like any other kid, I looked forward to the holidays for the few gifts I could depend on, but that happy anticipation was always tempered with anxiety over my mother's behavior.

Today, we know that there is a genetic predisposition to alcoholism and addiction, and I'm certain my mother had it. She grew up in a large farming family in the Blue Ridge Mountains of Virginia. Before and after Prohibition, "moonshining," or the illegal production of alcohol, was endemic to the culture throughout Appalachia. I don't know if my grandfather kept a still (I wouldn't be surprised), but he always had plenty of corn liquor and peach brandy. Later, one of my uncles did keep one. My mother, one of nine children, had four brothers and four sisters: every brother was an alcoholic, and all died by age 65; my mother was an alcoholic, and three of her four sisters drank heavily. Only one of the nine siblings didn't drink to excess.

The same pattern was true with tobacco. My grandfather, and later one of my uncles, was primarily a fruit farmer. But there were times when a grove of trees no longer bore fruit and would have to come out, often to be replaced by tobacco. Its cultivation was a fundamental part of the agricultural economy in Virginia at that time; and many fruit farmers diversified their crops by growing, harvesting, and curing it. My uncle had a curing barn to dry the leaves, and one of my keenest childhood memories was spending nights in there with my brother and cousins. We were

Michael D. Pratt

responsible for keeping a well-stoked fire in a woodstove and, to this day, I can't remember ever being hotter.

My grandfather, my mother, and all but one of her siblings smoked. My mother began when she was16 years old. Both my parents were chain smokers; I vividly remember watching them light cigarettes for each other from the ends of their still-burning ones. The same was true for all of my friends' parents. The only adult I knew who didn't smoke was the minister of my Southern Baptist church. (At least, I never saw him do it.) As a child, I knew I didn't like the smell of tobacco smoke; I knew it bothered my eyes and impaired my breathing, but I didn't know that my fairly regular ear infections and constant bronchial distress were the result of living in a smoke-filled home. When I was growing up during the1960s, concern about the hazards of smoking was only beginning to gain currency; second-hand smoke was not implicated in health issues.

It's not surprising, then, that this experience was the primary reason David's smoking was so appalling to me. It had contributed to the heart disease that killed my father at age 38; by age 50, my mother became a chronic emphysema sufferer, and was diagnosed with cancer in her mid-60s. Her surgeon told her that her only possibility for recovery required giving up smoking. His words were more effective than my chronic badgering. To my astonishment, she "cold turkeyed" and never had another puff. Alas, her lifestyle change came too late. She had an aggressive cancer that returned within three years; two years after the recurrence, she was dead. No matter how much I understood that she came from a tobacco-growing farm family, that my parents' generation knew little of the health risks of smoking, or that smoking was central to their culture, I found myself resentful of both my parents for engaging in a behavior that ultimately took them from me.

I might also have been inadvertently helped in my sober ways from earlier experiences. When I was very young, certainly not more than six, my grandfather asked me if I would like to try his chewing tobacco; I was only too glad to accept his offer. I've often wondered if his omission of instructions to spit out the tobacco and juice after chewing it was strategic. In any event, I swallowed it all and, in fairly short order, vomited violently. This event, coupled with the experience of living in a smoke-filled environment, left me with no interest in any form of tobacco.

I had a similar childhood experience with alcohol. In the fall of 1960, when I was a first grader, my Uncle Charles lived with my family. Of all my aunts and uncles, he suffered most severely from alcoholism. After school one day, I came home to find him watching the Yankees and Pirates in game seven of the World Series. This was my introduction to the Yankees—his favorite team and mine since that day—and to Jim Beam, his favorite bourbon. He offered me a sip and we passed the bottle back and forth. After Bill Mazeroski's home run stole victory from the Yankees, we continued to drink to console ourselves. My mother came home to discover us in tears and deep in our cups. This first encounter with alcohol, which left me thoroughly sick, would be my last until I was in college.

Alas, my Uncle Charles and my mother didn't benefit from the same lesson. My uncle had been discharged from the army during the Korean War for alcohol abuse. He spent most of the rest of his life a hopeless drunk, in and out of psychiatric wards, unable to work, and living with my grandparents. Unbelievably, in the wake of my grandfather's death in the late 1970s, Uncle Charles also "cold turkeyed" booze and cigarettes. Even though it's never clear precisely what causes an alcoholic to stop drinking, I have suspected that he felt responsible for my grandmother, and knew how much his dissolute lifestyle worried her.

Unlike Uncle Charles, who drank every day until he didn't, my mother was an occasional binge drinker. Her habit of drinking at times of celebration only intensified after my father died. I can't imagine the burden she must have felt raising five children—including a newborn—on her own, and with such meager means. Under the circumstances, it's probably understandable that she would turn to drink on an increasingly regular basis. But I began to dread coming home from school for fear I would find her drunk. Only rarely did I invite friends over, because I didn't want to risk the embarrassment. On several occasions, my older sister, Terri, who bore most of the burden of caring for our baby sister, would argue with my mother about her drinking. The pattern became painfully predictable: my siblings and I would arrive home from school, my sister would accuse my mother of being drunk, my mother would deny drinking and tell my sister to shut up and mind her own business, my sister would stomp off in tears, and I would retreat outside to play pick-up football or basketball.

I also experienced the emotional burden of being dependent upon a parent who, too often, was incapacitated. More than once I had to pick her up from the floor and help her into bed. Once she was so drunk that she mistook me for my father, already dead for four years. Regularly, I scouted cabinets for bottles of booze that I poured down the drain, in the vain hope that this would prevent the next binge. Years later, I engaged in the same sleuthing to prevent my son from using. That didn't work either.

When I became a Head of School, if I had known of children living in circumstances such as I had experienced, I would have been obligated to alert child protective services. I don't know if such an action would have affected my mother's behavior. Later, when she had dramatically curbed her drinking, she told me about a time when she became terribly depressed; it was as close as she ever came to acknowledging her alcoholism. By her account, I had wrenched her back into engagement by questioning why she took no interest in anything I did. It was likely little more than the typical adolescent, "But how about me?" challenge; but it somehow served to remind her that she was a mother with five children who needed her. I was surprised, and I suppose proud, that she credited me with pulling her out of her dark place.

So when many of my peers in high school took up smoking and ritualized drinking every weekend, I wanted no part of the scene. I had shared my experience with David in the hope that he, too, might choose to abstain. I was certainly aware of how damaging secrets are to every member of the family; even though I didn't want David to think ill of his grandmother, I believed it was important for him to know how destructive her alcoholism was to her, to me, and to my siblings. Maybe by being honest about our family, I thought, the cycle would not be replicated with David.

This was also the reason why I chose to share with him the gruesome details of his cousin's kidnapping and murder, which occurred in the spring just before our move to Los Angeles. My older brother's youngest son, Nathan, had begun to experiment with drugs as an adolescent, and ultimately was caught up in a drug deal that went bad. In retaliation for an unpaid debt, he was kidnapped from a party, driven to a field outside of the town where they lived, and shot execution style. For almost two weeks, his family didn't know what had happened. Initially, the police assumed he had run away, but eventually his body was found. His murderer and the murderer's accomplice were tried and convicted, but this was scant comfort for my brother and his family.

When I returned from Nathan's funeral, I spoke at a Menlo School assembly about this senseless loss. I hoped that my family's pain might convince even one student to avoid using drugs. Having already shared the story with David, I excused him from the assembly, because I thought it might be too painful for him to hear again in that context. Was this a mistake? Would it have been better for David to absorb the pain? Would this have caused him to abstain? I don't know.

****

Michael D. Pratt

Now, at Brentwood School, I was caught between two worlds: my family's crisis and my professional obligations. What should be my first loyalty: my child, or the school that I ran? Was it possible to do right by both?

I was very concerned that the case would bring notoriety to the school, could adversely impact admissions and fundraising, and render my leadership untenable. I believed that honor required me to offer my resignation to my Board chair, Richard Sandler. A remarkable man—balanced and thoughtful with impeccable integrity—he rejected my offer and assured me that we would get through the ordeal and that the school would be stronger.

I doubted very much that David had acted alone, but when I pressed him, he insisted that no other students were involved. While I had much to learn about substance abuse, I suspected that he was not being truthful; I knew that drinking and drug use among adolescents was often a social experience. In order for the disciplinary process and outcome to be viewed as legitimate, I knew that the incident needed to be fully investigated. To that end, I asked our Dean of Students to find out if any of David's friends had also done badly on the English exam. One student had, and, when I confronted him, he admitted to eating mushrooms with David that day.

Before the Honor Board convened to hear the two cases, I let the Dean of Students know of my determination to recuse myself from the proceedings. I explained that I had an inherent conflict of interest and would accept any recommendation the Honor Board made. I asked only that, if the consequence stopped short of expulsion, I be able to add conditions, such as mandatory testing to ensure that they remained sober.

I had no clear sense of how the Honor Board would rule. There was a myth in the school of "zero tolerance," and a pervasive hardline attitude. Interestingly, the student handbook at the time, and earlier, didn't use this term, and didn't call for automatic expulsion for an offense such as David's. I also knew that my predecessor had exercised discretion according to the circumstances. Because of my conflict, I had elected to give up that prerogative. I didn't know if the Honor Board would take into account that my son was new to the school, was a first time offender, and had confessed to his transgression. The night before the hearing, I told David I had decided to recuse myself from the proceedings, would do nothing to protect him from the consequence of his actions, and advised him to be fully honest and contrite. He was shocked that I wouldn't intercede on his behalf, but this proved to be the first in a number of instances in which Susan and I would have to draw the line.

The day of the hearing was excruciatingly long. Because the Honor Board included students, it convened at the end of the school day. No parent looks forward to finding out the outcome of a disciplinary hearing involving his or her child; and as I discovered when I myself had to convey difficult news, the impulse is to defend the child and ask for a milder consequence. Because of the peculiar circumstances of this case, as a parent, I had no one to whom to appeal.

After what seemed an interminable wait, the Dean of Students came to my office to report the Honor Board's decision: both boys would be suspended from school for the entire second semester, but would be able to attend extra-curricular activities—athletics events, concerts, etc.—in order to maintain relationships with their peers. Given the seriousness of the offense and the prevailing attitudes in the school, I had worried that they would be expelled; so I was relieved. I asked how the suspension would work, and the Dean explained that the boys could be home schooled, working with tutors and submitting their work to their Brentwood teachers to be assessed. I expressed concern that this would place an undue burden on the Brentwood teachers; but the Dean assured me that the school had ample experience with this arrangement because, over the years, there had been a number of students who missed significant time from school while pursuing acting careers. I was surprised, but grateful that David would be able to continue his education under the auspices of the school.

While Susan and I were relieved that this option was available, we weren't sure it was the best choice for David. He, in fact, didn't want to be home schooled, but instead preferred to transfer to a public school. We rejected that idea in part on educational grounds, but more because we were concerned that he would gravitate to the wrong peers. Norm Colb offered to readmit him at Menlo School, and the parents of one of his close friends there said he could live with them. Even though Susan and I were enormously grateful for these generous offers, we didn't want to visit our family's problems on others, and we were not at all confident that we could expect our son to abstain from alcohol and drugs. After considerable soul searching, we chose home schooling for David.

I was terribly naïve to assume that the school community would accept this resolution, even though the Dean of Students had assured me that the arrangement was not extraordinary. I called a meeting to inform the faculty of the Honor Board's judgment, and the resolution that both boys would be home schooled. I expressed gratitude to the Honor Board for their compassionate ruling, and to the teachers for their understanding and willingness to assess the boys' work. It would be an understatement to say that the faculty's reaction was stony silence.

At that point in my Headship, I didn't think it appropriate to communicate the details of disciplinary actions except to the families involved, out of concern for their privacy. I came to understand that the communications vacuum would be filled by rumor, which more often than not was far more damaging than the truth. I was reminded of the aphorism often attributed to Mark Twain: "A lie is halfway round the world before truth has got its boots on."

Certainly in this case, the rumors were malicious and widespread. Several days after I met with the faculty, the anonymous letter below was mailed to the entire parent body, except for Susan and me.

February 11, 2002

Dear Brentwood Parent:

It is with great disappointment and a sense of alarm that I write this letter today. When I arrived at school on February 6th, this is what I heard. During semester finals, two Brentwood students- one of them the son of Michael Pratt, the Brentwood School Headmaster, were caught having taken hallucinogenic mushrooms before a final exam. According to long-standing Brentwood policy, there is 'zero tolerance' for this infraction. Suspension is mandatory, which includes the offending Brentwood student not being involved in the school for the semester.

Michael Pratt called a mandatory assembly for all faculty on February 5, 2002 and here are the results. The Brentwood policy of zero tolerance is not going to be applied in this particular case. Instead, the students have 'chosen' to be home schooled by Brentwood faculty and will receive Brentwood School course credit. This modification is contrary to all past punishments and sets a new precedence in leniency and liability for the school.

I am a Brentwood parent and have been involved in the school since the 1980's. I have seen Brentwood grow in many ways, thanks to the many involved and caring families. The quality and stature of this institution has risen quickly to national prominence. And now, with this obviously discriminatory exception to the policy, this hard work by so many will be damaged. The integrity of the school will now be in question.

I am compelled to write to all parents and ask, "Is this what we want to teach our children?" We try to guide our children in the best manor we can and we expect from Brentwood that the school will also guide our children with honor and integrity. Now, we see that even though we read and agree to strictly follow the Brentwood principles, it turns out that signing the oath really doesn't mean a thing. How can our kids believe us if we say one thing and our school doesn't back itself or us? What does this teach them when they get out of school and have to fend for themselves?

We will now be spending our money for the faculty to home school these two students. They will be taking up time that should probably be given to the deserving students who have followed the rules. The morale of the faculty will most certainly be damaged and retaining quality teachers will be a problem when it is known that the Headmaster will selectively not back them and the school's policy. And the message to our children will be: if you have connections, then you can get away with whatever you want. How will every other student view this? Ask your children what they think.

If the disciplinary committee has approved this, then shame on them. If the Board of Directors has approved this, then shame on all of them and shame on Michael Pratt for not upholding Brentwood School's policies to the established standards before his personal crisis. We all would like to think that we have a Headmaster who would have risen to this personal and professional challenge. Clearly, he did not.

The real question is: are we going to uphold Brentwood's policies and standards? I hope that many of you will see this as a time to talk--and act.

A very concerned Brentwood Parent

The letter was shot through with inaccuracies, speculation, innuendo, and outright lies. Worst of all, it was anonymous, which made responding to it very difficult.

Cultures in which there is denial, lack of trust, and fear of retribution invite this sort of corrosive behavior.

The great irony is that I had been at such pains to preserve the credibility, integrity, and honor of the school by having already offered my resignation, recused myself from the proceedings, and given up the normal benefit of the Head's review and final decision based on the recommendation and any extenuating circumstances deemed relevant.

The letter's contention had not a shred of truth, but I understood that I could not simply ignore it and depend on the good faith and trust of the community. I asked Board Chair Richard Sandler to call a special Board meeting to determine the best way to respond. As had been the case throughout the crisis, he handled the matter with the utmost skill and discretion. The Board determined that the matter should be investigated and that a letter should be sent to the school community detailing the results. Ultimately, that investigation and the subsequent letter made clear I had recused myself from the proceedings and had accepted in full the Honor Board's recommendation. With this, the immediate crisis in my leadership had passed, but the crisis in my family was only beginning.

Rehab

Fear, confusion, and self-reproach were several of the many states of mind that Susan and I went through in the days after David's suspension. Why had he done something so at odds with our values, so dangerous and self-destructive, so disrespectful of my position in the school—in short, so outside of his character as we understood it?

Growing up, David had been a very easy child. There were no birth difficulties, and his early years passed normally and happily. He made friends easily; flourished in elementary school; and participated in sports, clubs, and music. He was an early reader and was able to entertain himself for long periods with toys and Legos. He was certainly excitable, and Susan often noticed that too much sugar raised that level even further. She believed we'd have to keep a close watch on him as he moved into adolescence, because he might be similarly susceptible to alcohol and drugs. Nonetheless, we were shocked when we found out about his drug use. Years later, we learned that when he was in middle school he occasionally sneaked sips of liquor when we were out for an evening.

In those early days, we allowed ourselves to hope that he'd simply made a colossally stupid error in judgment, and that from now on he'd take his medicine, move forward, and be productive. We had him continue with the same therapist, and also decided to have his learning style evaluated. We knew he was very bright, and while we didn't place much emphasis on grades, we believed he was a chronic underperformer. In fact, he put very little effort into his academics and was content to do just enough to get by. He summed up his attitude in this pithy admission: "B's are my friends." His evaluation revealed what we'd expected: David was highly intelligent, and his performance at school didn't reflect his ability. It also indicated that he suffered from significant ADHD. This explained a number of his behaviors: procrastination, disorganization, poor focus, and impulsivity—all adding up to impaired performance.

As an educator, I'd seen this profile many times before, and statistics bear out my experience: even though estimates vary, it's likely that 5-16% of school-aged children are affected by ADHD, and the incidence among boys is two to four times more common than among girls. I had seen parents pull out their hair in frustration. Why was their perfectly bright son so lazy? Why didn't he care more about his performance? Why couldn't he see that his lack of effort would seriously erode his opportunity to attend a good college?

I suppose I was relieved to learn that David's inattention wasn't the product of willfulness or laziness. I was concerned, however, because the most effective pharmaceutical therapy to treat ADHD is a stimulant—essentially speed—and that, given his drug experimentation, providing him a drug he could abuse would be a terrible idea. I was all too aware that some adolescent ADHD sufferers turned to drugs in an effort to self-medicate their symptoms. I wondered if this was true in our son's case. Perhaps had we known of his condition earlier, we could have treated him pharmaceutically, and he might not have turned to drug abuse. I've looked back with a deep sense of irony: despite our long careers in education, Susan and I weren't able to recognize David's classic ADHD symptoms.

Just as many difficulties come unbidden, so, at times, does help. In the midst of our worries about the deeper meaning of our son's behavior, I got a call from a recent acquaintance who is a prominent drug counselor. Betty Wyman had contacted me shortly after my arrival at Brentwood to introduce herself and to let me know that she'd be pleased to be a resource for any of our students in need of help. After word of David's trouble reached her, she called again to urge that we consider having him meet with a drug counselor. At this point, we didn't assume he was an addict, but we also believed there was nothing to lose in having him assessed. His therapist agreed, since David had no deep psychological issues. On Betty's advice, we arranged for him to meet with Jim Earnhardt, who would play a crucial role in our son's life for the next year and a half.

****

Having made some decisions about the approach to David's therapy, we turned our attention to his education. After several conversations with the mother of the student who was involved in the mushroom-eating episode, we jointly agreed to hire a tutor who would meet with both boys in our home. Their Brentwood teachers provided the course materials, the tutor instructed them, and their teachers assessed the work. We also felt that, since they loved music, the boys could take the time to attend a music theory class at a community college. We reasoned that the experience would be positive, and it wouldn't hurt to get college credit.

Virtually the entire burden of overseeing the home schooling and transportation to the community college fell on Susan, who was still maintaining an active professional presence in San Francisco. It would have been hard enough to oversee two adolescent boys on a daily basis, but David's attitude made the situation excruciating. Despite causing the disruption in his and our lives, he felt he should be allowed to make decisions about his own education. When we exercised our better judgment, he was grumpy and uncooperative, and continued his practice of doing the bare minimum to get by. He did the same with the community college course, including cutting class frequently and failing to turn in assignments. Sitting through a three-hour class that he regarded as uninteresting and unimportant was a recipe for disaster. When we learned about his irresponsible behavior, we cracked down, and he did enough work to complete the course satisfactorily. He finished the home schooling in good standing, including strong performances on his two Advanced Placement exams.

Even without having to handle his day-to-day issues, this period was nearly impossible for me, personally and professionally. Like any other parent whose child has been removed from school, I was both worried and embarrassed. I hoped that our son would bounce back quickly and learn from the difficult experience he'd brought upon himself, but I couldn't be certain he wouldn't descend further. I was committed to being as open and dignified as possible, but the subject was awkward. I wasn't just any parent whose child had been suspended; I was the public face of the school.

David's actions isolated him, and in subtle ways, me as well. My colleagues, students, and other parents didn't know how to respond. Should they ask after him, or just pretend the event had never occurred? For the most part, this is precisely what happened. There were occasional exceptions, both negative and positive. Susan and I were stunned into silence at a dinner party when another parent, well into his cups and in a weak attempt at humor, made a snide remark about the Head of School's druggie son. On the other hand, I received an anonymous note from a student—clearly a girl—expressing her sympathy for David's difficulty and the impact of his suspension on our family. The note also expressed gratitude for the dignified way I'd carried myself throughout the crisis. Even though it was difficult, I decided to read it at an upper school assembly, both to thank the anonymous author and also to demonstrate my willingness to be open in front of the community.

David's relationship with drug therapist Jim Earnhardt was, as is typical, confidential. We had an understanding that there would be occasional status reports. We took no news as good news, but we certainly worried about the meaning of our son's attitude about home schooling. We'd hoped he would see his experience as an opportunity to understand himself better and to set healthy priorities. Instead, he was belligerent, sullen, and resentful.

We also felt it was important for David to be on a shorter leash. He socialized considerably less than before the suspension, but we did permit him to participate in enrichment activities. He attended Alcoholics Anonymous meetings and continued his guitar lessons. After one evening's lesson, he called to say he'd had a car wreck: he wasn't hurt, but the car was seriously damaged. I met him at the scene of the accident. He said he'd rounded a curve too fast, swung wide, and plowed into the rear of a parked truck. He'd obviously been driving recklessly, so I asked him if he was high, but he denied having taken anything. I told him this was a good thing, since we'd have to call the police to report the wreck. As it happens, a neighbor had already done so, and they soon appeared. To this day, I remain astonished by their response. They did no field sobriety tests and didn't charge David with reckless driving. The consequence was that he totaled an almost new car, lost his driving privileges for a period, and our insurance rates went up.

Our discussion about the car wreck followed a familiar pattern. Though he was shaken by the incident and no doubt upset that he couldn't drive, he seemed totally unreflective. To him, it appeared to be just one more thing to get through, not anything that required soul searching or change of behavior. I, on the other hand, believed that his behavior was willful, and was terribly upset that he'd act so recklessly. I also believed that if I said just the right thing, in just the right way, everything would click and he'd put the train back on the rails. I begged him to look deeply at his behavior and to think about what sort of person he wanted to be. He'd violated a school policy and been suspended; he was dragging his feet with the home schooling and was regularly disrespectful to his mother, who had turned her life inside out to make the home schooling possible. And now he'd totaled a car. He gave no response, other than "um-hmm, um-hmm, um-hmm." I suspect that he actually couldn't explain his behavior, and that he just wanted the conversation to end.

Not long after, my frustration with his attitude and behavior exploded during dinner. As usual, he was sullen throughout the meal, complained about the food, and was short with Susan. I leapt from my chair, shaking with pent-up rage. Susan did her best to de-escalate the situation; but I was so angry I could hardly see straight and, at the same time, deeply remorseful for losing control.

This incident is seared into my memory as an expression of my limitations. I also came to understand that I had to alter my attitudes. Haranguing, moralizing, and angrily threatening were of no value. I was beginning to comprehend the obvious: it was essential to articulate boundaries and expectations clearly and for consequences to be measured and certain. In truth, this had always been a struggle for me. I'd been overindulgent of David, perhaps because, after age 12, I'd had no father to support and guide me. Susan was much quicker to shorten the leash, which inevitably made her the "bad cop" to my "good cop," and exacerbated her difficulties in managing the home schooling. Gradually I was coming to see that my natural instincts to help, to understand, and to fix, were part of the problem.

The school year ended and, with summer beginning, we felt it was important for David to have some structure. He was continuing with his therapy, but we knew that being otherwise unoccupied wouldn't be good. Through school friends, I found him an internship in a music production company, which, as a budding musician, he knew was a great opportunity. I was working on setting better boundaries, but was still unable to resist being overly helpful.

With this new work, we allowed David to drive by himself again. One day not long after, he came home to tell us the car had been damaged in the parking lot and no note had been left. In fact, along the driver's side from front to back, there was a crease in the metal. Though his story was plausible, I was skeptical, thinking it was more likely he'd scraped the car and lied to cover it up. A 1970 Mercedes-Benz, the car's only virtue was its great looks; it, too, was now totaled. Some time later, he admitted that he was high and had, in fact, scraped the car.

David's older sister, Margaret, with whom he was very close, had recently graduated from University of California, Berkeley, and was working in the campus library. We all agreed that he could spend a few days with her. This time was a welcome respite for Susan and me; in truth, we were relieved to have him under someone else's watchful eye, and we had the utmost confidence in Margaret.

When he returned, we immediately knew something was wrong, and he asked if we could talk. He told us that, while Margaret was at work, he'd purchased a bottle of cough syrup, drunk the entire bottle, and had a very bad reaction. His sister had given him twenty-four hours to tell us before she would do so. Reeling, we asked him why he had done such a thing. He said he'd had an urge to get high, and knew that cough syrup would work. David learned on the Internet that many cough suppressants contain dextromethorphan, or DXM, which is hallucinogenic when taken above therapeutic levels. This was news to us.

This latest turn was profoundly difficult to process. Again, the character questions. How could he put his sister in such a position? Didn't he care about anyone? Were his pleasures more important to him than anything or anybody? Could he not see that his behaviors showed the deepest disrespect to his values? And, of course, the deeper question: was he an addict?

In time we'd come to understand that David's behavior was not simply a matter of adolescent defiance or disregard for the people who loved him most. This incident made clear that the episode that had gotten him removed from school wasn't a single instance of poor judgment, and that stronger intervention would be necessary.

We contacted his drug counselor, who agreed to meet with him right away. His assessment was that David was an addict and recommended that we place him in an inpatient rehab facility.

I felt as if I'd been punched in the stomach. Like most parents, I couldn't easily accept that my child was an addict. Despite having grown up with an alcoholic mother, I didn't know anything about the disease of addiction, and wondered how long the "cure" would take. I knew our health insurance didn't cover inpatient drug rehabilitation, and I didn't know how we could afford the intervention. We'd already spent what to us was a small fortune on drug counseling, learning specialists, and tutors.

But on the therapist's recommendation, I contacted Visions, an adolescent drug rehabilitation facility that had recently opened in Malibu. After some discussion about the treatment, the director and I agreed on a fee, and he offered to meet off site so that Susan and I could better understand the facility and the treatment plan. Heads of School by nature are problem solvers, so I wanted to know about success rates. I was aghast when the response was that relapse was typically part of the recovery process. When I pressed, he said that approximately 25% of adolescents who go through rehab don't relapse, another 50% have at least one relapse and often require additional stays in residential treatment, and another 25% never recover. I wanted very much to be optimistic and believe that David would be among the lucky 25%, but the odds seemed daunting, and I was beginning to comprehend that we were likely in this for the long haul. We really felt we had no option, so we agreed to place David in residential treatment. Later, I learned that the odds are actually more staggering: fully 83% of addicts relapse within a year of entering rehab.

Like most such centers, Visions placed heavy restrictions on patients, including limiting communication. David was in treatment with four other adolescents, a mix of boys and girls, who were addicted to alcohol and a variety of drugs. Unlike our son, most were also being treated pharmaceutically for depression and other psychological conditions. After a week, we were allowed to visit him and, after a brief hello, the first words out of his mouth were, "I want a drink so badly." I was shocked, first by the fact that this was paramount in his mind, and second that it was alcohol he wanted. I knew he had eaten mushrooms and smoked marijuana; I knew about the cough syrup episode. But I didn't know he drank. Years later he told me he'd stolen from our liquor cabinet throughout his suspension from school. He'd also eaten large quantities of nutmeg in order to experience hallucinations. He timed his drug tests, used other people's urine, and flushed his system with large quantities of water to avoid detection. Today my naiveté seems mind boggling, but parents can't really comprehend a child's addiction until they experience it.

Weekly family days are typical in treatment programs. They're opportunities to meet individually with therapists to learn how the treatment for their loved one is going, to come together with the other families as a support group, and to gather with the residents and their families. Our first one was eye opening. David's therapist told us that his addiction was deep and serious and that he would get high on anything available. We were advised that addicts are clever at concealing their use and that we should purge our home of any mood-altering substances. When we got home, we gave away our wine and liquor, poured out concentrated lemon juice (yes, it contains alcohol), threw away nutmeg and all cough medications, and went through David's things with a fine-toothed comb. His counselor even told us to look behind the electrical cover plates throughout the house, which I did.

One of the strongest ethics in addiction treatment is that what's said in a group setting remains in strict confidence. I was surprised, then, to discover that I was a folk hero of sorts among the other parents, who apparently had learned I'd recused myself from the Honor Board hearing that resulted in David's suspension from school. I was reminded that Los Angeles thrives on gossip, and somehow word of our experience had spread to parents who had no affiliation at all with the school.

We were the most recent members of the group and were shocked by the struggles the other parents had experienced with their children. Living with David for the previous six months had pushed us to our emotional limits, but we were now hearing that others had it worse; we hadn't faced the extremes of blatant disrespect and defiance that most of the others had. In this initial session, both those traits were in full view, as several of the residents—one girl in particular—used language that would have caused the saltiest sailor to blush. I was certain that her parents hadn't raised her in a way to lead to such disrespect. Parent after parent spoke about how alcohol and drugs had transformed their sweet and kind child into an ill-behaved, disrespectful stranger in their home. Susan and I were beginning to ask ourselves if we really knew our son, and where we'd gone wrong. Guilt mingles with grief in every parent of an addicted child. We heard in this first group meeting that we didn't cause his addiction, and we couldn't cure it. This is very difficult for any parent to accept, because we are conditioned to feel responsible for how our children turn out.

The most difficult moment of the day for us was David's request to be allowed to smoke while in treatment. When we balked, his counselor pointed out that every other resident smoked, and that it made sense to focus on the larger issue. Reluctantly, we agreed, which meant that we were providing our child with cigarettes. It may be true that parents don't cause their children's addiction, but I now felt complicit in a habit with devastating health consequences. If I had the decision to make over again, I don't know what it would be; but I do think that adolescent treatment centers should not permit smoking.

During the group meetings, and even during the limited time that David was permitted to visit with us outside the treatment center, he was guarded and taciturn. Of course, Susan and I were anxious and eager to know how he was doing; later on we'd realize that he felt we were interrogating him. He had hidden so much from us for months that it was now difficult for him to open up. He also felt under intense pressure to seem okay, when he was anything but. From our point of view, we wanted openness so that we could begin to trust him and to heal. Alas, what we wanted and needed, he couldn't give.

After David's release from rehab, his godfather, Bob Trammell, offered him a great opportunity to join him on a canoe trip to the Adirondacks. Bob and I had met when we were in eighth grade and, as a fellow teetotaler in high school, he and I naturally became best friends. We roomed together in college and later remained close despite living far apart. When David was born, we asked him to be his godfather, and it was a role Bob took very seriously.

The two had been on a camping and canoe trip together before, so Bob thought another one might be good for David. Susan and I agreed, thinking he'd benefit from the physical challenge, would be safe with Bob, and that it was important for him to have caring adults in his life other than his parents.

The time with Bob was therapeutic. Bob told us David had opened up about his cravings and discussed his strategies for resisting temptations, which included meditation. This was an area in which Bob was deeply experienced, so he reinforced its benefits for David and encouraged him to stick with the practice.

This trip, in conjunction with his recent rehab, gave us reason for a great deal of hope, but we also felt trepidation. We hoped that David was "cured," or at least equipped to resist the many temptations that would surround him. We hoped also that he'd be able to re-enter school with renewed focus and a determination to acquit himself well, so as to earn back the trust he'd broken the year before. Coupled with this hope was the terrible fear that he wouldn't make it—that he'd relapse, and continue his downward spiral. In accepting the position at Brentwood, I'd moved my family from a happy, settled life in the hope that I'd advance myself professionally and also be able to provide an excellent education for my son. He'd already been removed from school; now I worried that he'd relapse, and I'd have no choice but to expel him. I'd already determined that if this happened, I'd resign, bringing my career as a Head of School to an end. The stakes were high.

Relapse

David had missed the second semester of his junior year, but so had we. All parents want to take pride in their child's accomplishments and share in the joys they experience. At every school concert, play, or athletic contest I attended, I lamented that this was not part of my son's experience. I'd spent my career in education so I could make a difference in the lives of adolescents. I spent my days creating educational circumstances under which they could flourish, and took great joy in watching them take advantage of so many opportunities. So naturally I wanted desperately for David to flourish as well. Though colored by much doubt, I devoutly hoped that his senior year would mark a turning point in his life.

The fall of 2002 began well enough, though he chose not to play football. I understood, since we'd previously agreed this was his decision, but it was still one I regretted. However he used his time, I just wanted him to take himself seriously and be productive. His classroom performance was adequate. He earned A's and B's, and his teachers didn't complain about a poor attitude or work ethic. I came to accept that he wouldn't push himself academically and would participate only minimally in school life. I knew it would be much better for David if he committed himself fully, but I couldn't make that commitment for him.

His life was simple: go to school, do some homework, go to Alcoholics Anonymous meetings, take guitar lessons, and practice with his rock band. Happily, David made good friends, including the members of his band, all fellow

Brentwood students. I hoped this experience would have a positive influence on him.

Like every other student at Brentwood, David signed up for classes that would make him competitive for college admissions, took his SATs, filled out college applications, and hoped for the best. Of course, the C- from his first semester in junior English—the result of his inability to complete his mid-year exam—and his subsequent suspension, affected his options. For many Brentwood parents, or independent school parents generally, this would have seemed tragic. For Susan and me, where he would attend college was the least of our concerns—we had gained a hard-earned perspective. There are countless good colleges, and the quality of the education is commensurate with the student's effort. The more important question was our son's health—literally a matter of life and death. We understood that good things would happen as long as he stayed sober, and bad things would happen—things much worse than failing to get into a top college—if he didn't. When he got into several of the universities in the University of California system, we were relieved, and felt he'd taken an important step in his journey back to a healthy, productive life.

Beyond the outward signs of health—performance in his classes and maintaining his friends and interests—we really didn't know how David was doing. He remained taciturn and shared very little with us. Having worked with adolescents throughout my professional life, I knew that they don't typically share much of their inner life with their parents. In fact, I'd often advised parents to accept the abbreviated conversations and monosyllabic responses as a developmental inevitability as their child became more independent. But Susan and I worried that the reason he had so little to say was because he had so much to hide. In fact, he did have a lot to hide. He had used throughout his senior year and had developed a variety of ways to defeat the testing. Lies and deception are a heavy burden. At that time, we thought he was struggling to stay sober. If only that had been the case.

That spring, David's counselor suggested we have a family check-in. I always went into these meetings with a mixture of hope and trepidation. This time, we shared that we wished he'd be more open and that, in order for us to trust that he was sticking with his program and was making progress in his recovery, we needed him to be more transparent. For his part, David complained that we seemed to need constant proof that he was fine, and that such pressure was hard for him to endure; in fact, it actually made him want to use. We would learn in time that statements of this sort are the addict's stock-in-trade: blame someone else, anyone else, for the alcohol and substance abuse.

He demanded to know why we couldn't just trust him. We knew from our Al-Anon and family meetings that addicts are masters in emotional manipulation, and we began to see his criticizing our lack of trust for what it was. David's behavior had eroded that trust. While it was important for us to be open to his efforts to make progress in his recovery, it was his responsibility to regain our trust, which would require greater openness. We certainly didn't require a daily blow-by-blow account of what he was thinking and how he was feeling, but we did need to hear from him that he was dedicated to his program and that he wanted to be sober.

Our meeting intensified our concern that he wasn't really committed to sobriety, but rather just white-knuckling his way to the end of the school year. His counselor told us that David admitted he'd snorted ground-up NoDoz tablets. Interestingly, the counselor also said he wasn't overly concerned about the large dose of caffeine since, like many recovering addicts, David consumed large amounts of coffee. It was the way he'd ingested the caffeine that was a cause for concern.

Our worry that he wasn't doing well in recovery increased a short time later. David spent part of his spring break with a friend in Northern California. While there, he met with one of his former Menlo School teachers, himself a recovering alcoholic, who later told me he was sure our son wasn't done using. When I pressed him to explain why, he told me that David had said he couldn't imagine never drinking again. I certainly understood that alcoholics couldn't say they'll never take another drink, but I was heartbroken to learn that he couldn't even imagine a sober life.

Our trust was further eroded when we found out he was still smoking. After his stay in residential treatment ended, he agreed to try to quit; and we purchased Nicorette so he could wean himself from tobacco. He finally admitted that he hadn't actually used the product, arguing that he liked to smoke, that it was his body, and he didn't see why we couldn't accept this. Having grown up in a home filled with smoke, and having lost a father to heart disease and a mother to cancer, I couldn't accept that my child would so cavalierly engage in a habit with such dire health consequences. The problem was that David was capable only of considering his immediate pleasure, not the long-term consequences of his behavior. He had no fear that alcohol, cigarettes, or any other drug could do irreparable harm.

In his final couple of months of high school, we knew he was barely clinging to abstinence. We were reduced to hoping that the prospect of college would be sufficient motivation to remain sober.

For Heads of School, the end of the school year is always intensely busy. In addition to running the usual day-to-day events, completing initiatives, and planning for the next year, there are all of the final games, plays, awards assemblies, and ceremonies—including graduation—to attend. This is a time when seniors and their parents experience pride and nostalgia. Since David had essentially checked out from the midpoint of his junior year, I suspect he was simply glad it was over. For my part, I felt more relief than pride. At commencement, I awarded him his diploma, hugged him, and thought to myself: at least he made it.

It seemed to me that, by any objective standard, David had a lot to look forward to: he'd gotten a summer job in the music industry; his band had several gigs lined up, including a show at the Roxy the night of graduation; and he'd be heading off to college in the fall. What further motivation did he need to stay sober?

On graduation night, the band played a strong set, and Susan and I headed home, pleased that David was proud of the performance. A couple of days later, he started his summer job. With each passing day, he seemed increasingly edgy. He also looked especially thin. Over the past couple of years, as he got taller, he'd gradually lost his baby fat. The recent weight loss, however, seemed precipitous, and was accompanied by an outbreak of severe acne, which seemed oddly timed, since he'd made it through most of adolescence with little more than an occasional pimple. In short, he didn't look healthy.

In early July 2003, soon after his 18th birthday, David's drug counselor scheduled a family meeting, which we assumed would be a new status report. It was: David had relapsed, this time on crystal methamphetamine. He had failed a drug test earlier in the summer and was warned that another "dirty" test would mean that we would have to be told. Despite this warning, David was unable to resist his new obsession. We later found out that a kid he'd met in rehab the previous summer had turned him on to the substance.

I'm not sure why I was surprised by the new revelation, but I was. I'd been so hopeful that he'd gotten himself back on track. I somehow had rationalized the edginess, the weight loss, and the poor complexion. My hope had blinded me to what was right in front of me. Susan and I were shaken to our cores. This was no longer drinking some beer or smoking a joint. He had now turned to hard drugs. Where would this end?

Michael D. Pratt

The counselor had convinced David to go back into rehab, and urged us to support this decision. He recommended Cirque Lodge, a high-end treatment center for adults in Utah. Again we benefitted from a deep discount, without which we wouldn't have been able to afford treatment, since our insurance covered only limited outpatient care. Susan and I agreed to pay $5,000 toward the cost, and David would owe an equal amount. We doubted he'd be able to repay this money, but since he was now 18, we felt his debts were his responsibility.

We found ourselves in a situation so many families face: our child had a deadly disease, and we didn't know if we could afford the treatment. Inpatient care is dauntingly expensive, typically $1,000 or more per day. Most insurance companies cover only 30 days, if anything. Many experts in drug treatment don't believe this is an adequate length of time, but rehabilitation centers have created 30-day programs based on insurance limitations. These factors often mean that many addicts get limited or no treatment. The economic and social costs of this gap in healthcare are staggering: in 2006, the Centers for Disease Control and Prevention estimated that alcoholism had a $223.5 billion dollar adverse impact; drug use adds to this cost.[1] To say nothing of the heartache that families suffer when addiction of a loved one goes untreated.

David had turned 18 only a week before returning to rehab, and our attitude toward both his treatment and responsibilities shifted dramatically. We loved him no less; we agonized over his health no less; we hoped for his future no less. But now he was legally an adult, and should be responsible for his own debts, and answerable for his conduct. We had provided him every advantage—a loving family, an excellent education, travel, music lessons—to be successful. Now his successes would depend on his own initiative.

As is typical of inpatient treatment, David was to stay a month at Cirque Lodge. It was terribly painful putting him on a plane and sending him away from us for that long. At the same time, we were relieved that he'd be in treatment, where he'd be safe and drug free. We discovered that our sense of relief is a common experience for families of addicts; we can relax and live our own lives, even if briefly, while the addict is in treatment. Their destructive behaviors, manipulations, and sullen attitudes are, for a while, someone else's problem.

In Al-Anon, one also learns that addiction is a family disease, because the addict's behavior impacts the entire family. It's vital for the family to continue to love the addict and to support him or her by drawing very clear boundaries. Even though Susan and I had already attended many Al-Anon meetings, we knew we had a great deal more to learn. We understood that the more we found out about addiction, the more helpful we could be to our son. To signal our support and to deepen our understanding, we decided that we would attend a family weekend midway through his Cirque Lodge stay.

Our time there couldn't have been more eye opening. The facility is certainly among the most highly regarded rehabilitation centers in the country. Settled in a beautiful area in Utah, nothing is spared to aid in recovery: delicious and healthy food, group sessions led by highly skilled counselors, personal therapists, medical staff trained in recovery, equine therapy, and high-end amenities. During family weekends, visitors attend group sessions together—with and without the residents—as well as sessions with the residents and their personal counselors, equine therapy, and educational sessions, all designed to help families understand that alcohol and drug addiction is a disease.

In truth, I had always viewed addiction as a character flaw or destructive willfulness. I was surprised to find out that, since 1956, the American Medical Association has classified alcoholism as a disease. Today, 40 million Americans suffer from alcohol and drug problems, and addiction is now understood to be a complex brain disease, rather than a lack of willpower.[2] Like other diseases, this terrible afflic-tion is progressive and will ultimately take the sufferer's life unless it's treated successfully. Unlike other diseases, there's no surgery or drug therapy (at least so far) that results in a "cure." The best the addict can hope for is to live per-manently in recovery, which simply means not using any addictive substance, but only approximately 10% of those afflicted receive treatment.

The hardest aspect of this disease, and recovery from it, for me to understand was the phenomenon of relapse. I remembered being told, before David's first rehab, that only 25% of those initially going in enjoy long-term recov-ery. Our son was now back because he'd relapsed on a drug—methamphetamine—that was far more dangerous than what he'd used before. I asked his counselor what the recovery rate was from meth, and was disheartened to hear the answer: 9%. All this time, money, and immeasurable anguish, and David had less than a one-in-ten chance to recover.

But why is relapse so commonly part of the recovery process? The simple answer is that the addict becomes physically and psychologically dependent on mood-alter-ing substances. Setting aside the reason for trying alcohol and drugs in the first place—after all, very few people go through their lives never taking so much as a sip of alco-hol or a puff of a cigarette—those who are predisposed to addiction derive enormous pleasure from these chemicals. I've heard addicts say many times that, when they first used alcohol or drugs, they finally felt normal or were euphoric. Naturally, these users want to repeat those feelings; but over time, their brains require more and more of the sub-stance to get the same feeling, so all of their efforts become focused on obtaining more.

Meth is a particular scourge. Produced from readily available chemicals, it's inexpensive, highly addictive, and physically debilitating. Meth users eventually develop ter-rible skin lesions, lose their teeth from depleted enamel, lose weight, are unable to sleep, become paranoid, and suffer brain damage. Despite the consequences, the drug is compelling. It's a stimulant that affects the central nervous system by releasing and blocking the re-uptake of dopamine in the brain. David once explained to me that when he used, he was intensely happy, and felt he was capable of achieving anything. Even menial tasks such as vacuuming the floor were fun and engaging.

For a non-addict, the bad consequences of overindulgence send a simple message: don't do that again. For the addict, the lesson isn't so simple. This is why we often hear that, for recovery to be sustainable, the addict must hit bottom. This is the moment when the addict accepts that the consequences of using—the loss of a job, the loss of family and friends, involvement with the police, and even death—exceeds the temporary pleasure derived from alcohol and drugs. For Susan and me, the question was, what would it take for David to hit bottom, and would it happen before he killed himself or someone else?

I hadn't seen evidence that any action we'd taken or anything we'd said had had any impact, something that was particularly difficult for either of us to understand. As educators, we believed deeply in the power of modeling, but also in the power of language. Once again we found ourselves thinking, "If only we could say the right thing to our son at the right time, in the right way, the light would surely switch on for him." To our shared frustration, this hadn't happened. No matter how many times we explained that his behaviors weren't acceptable to us and were self-destructive, he continued to use.

Yet an important aspect of this therapy is for family members to share with the addict the personal impact of the use. I'd never done this with David. I'd certainly been clear that I deplored his use but, aside from my explosion at the dinner table the previous summer, I'd mostly avoided showing anger or hurt. Now, during our Cirque Lodge family weekend, not only were we asked to tell him how we'd experienced his addiction in the presence of all the residents and their families, but we were also asked to speak first. I don't know whether this was a random choice, or if the counselors thought we seemed balanced and articulate. It may have been that they doubted that we (especially I) could maintain a detached calm, and believed that direct, raw sharing would make a difference. David looked horrified at the prospect.

The three of us sat in a triangle facing each other, encircled by the counselors, the other residents, and their families. Throughout the ordeal of David's alcohol and drug use, I had tried to avoid showing anger or causing him to feel guilty. I understood that he alone was responsible for using, but I alone was responsible for my feelings. I worried that if he were burdened by my feelings, it might get in the way of his recovery. Now, confronted with having to share my feelings within this group context, I was determined to maintain my composure and to state my feelings dispassionately, but I was unable to get past "David," before I broke down in tears. As I pressed on, Susan and David also began to cry. Susan spoke next, but David chose not to. He later told me that the exchange had been especially difficult for him because he'd never seen me cry, which made me wonder if I had made a mistake by being too guarded, too dispassionate, too detached. Had I somehow conveyed to our son that his behavior didn't really affect me?

Before leaving Cirque Lodge, we had a family meeting with David's personal counselor, who explained that our son had engaged willingly and openly in the program, and was beginning to develop a concept of a sober life. He also reminded us that recovery is a process and there was no guarantee he wouldn't slip again. I didn't want to hear the cautionary note. I wanted desperately to believe that, after his personal suffering, and with the benefit of two rehabilitation residencies and ongoing counseling, he was now in a sustainable recovery.

Susan and I had driven to Utah; given the distressing summer we'd experienced, we decided to take a brief detour on our way home to stay at Zion National Park in the southern part of the state. In the presence of indescribable natural grandeur, I felt a rush of conflicting emotions—feelings of grief for David's lost time, comingled with gratitude for the kindness of all those who had helped us, and hope that our son was finally back on track. He would be at Cirque Lodge for two more weeks, a time during which we could relax in the knowledge that he was safe and was getting the best treatment available.

The day he came back home, we picked him up from the airport and tried not to grill him with questions or look searchingly at him for clues of his condition—though we were relieved that he seemed markedly better. After a month of no meth or any other substance, his complexion looked healthy, he'd put on some much-needed weight, and was calm. We were having a friend over for dinner that first evening and, when David asked if he could go out, we agreed as long as he first greeted our guest and didn't stay out late. Our friend later commented on how good he looked; we were all glad that he seemed healthy and appeared to have made great progress in rehab. True to his word, David returned after a couple of hours, spoke briefly to the three of us, and then went to his room.

Later, as Susan and I were cleaning up in the kitchen, David came back downstairs looking like a zombie. He said he was sorry, but that he'd used meth. He was terribly embarrassed and felt that he'd failed. I felt as if I were suffocating. After two rehabs, he couldn't maintain his sobriety for 12 hours. Never in my life had I felt so helpless and hopeless. We told David to go to his room, and we would discuss the next steps in the morning.

Susan and I were numb. We agreed to call Jim Earnhardt (David's Los Angeles counselor) the next day to see what he advised. I took David's car keys from him and hid them, along with ours, so he couldn't leave during the night. Terribly concerned for his safety, I also inventoried every chemical in the garage and hid anything that could be inhaled. For the first time in this ordeal, I understood I couldn't trust him, because he couldn't trust himself. I also understood that he wasn't acting willfully; he was simply unable to control his behavior. I remain convinced that he didn't want to use meth that night, but he didn't have the capacity to resist.

The next morning we spoke with Jim, who urged us to call Cirque Lodge to see if they'd take David back. They agreed he could return for an evaluation, and we put him on the next flight to Utah. A few days later, his counselors advised us to place him in a nearby rehab facility for an indefinite period. We took a deep breath and ultimately agreed.

It was now clear that David wouldn't be starting college in the fall, if ever. Rather, he was starting his third rehab in little more than a year's time, with no end in sight. We wouldn't be paying college tuition; but since he'd begun his drug use, the tutoring, counseling, and rehab had easily cost us the equivalent of two years of higher education. I suspect any parent wouldn't begrudge an expense that would help their child, but we'd come to wonder if a third rehab was simply throwing good money after bad.

Susan flew to Utah to make arrangements for him to stay indefinitely at Journeys, a long-term care facility that also maintained sober living homes. We didn't know how long he'd be there or when we'd next see him. At this point, we were bleeding money, and could only hope that the rehab would make a difference. Perhaps the third time would be the charm. At least for now we could relax, knowing that David was safe.

Middle Ground

The past year and a half had been a nightmare and had taken a great toll on us. So often Susan and I expressed our gratitude to each other that our marriage was strong and that we'd been able to support each other through the ordeal. But, typical of families who deal with an addict, we were exhausted. Not only had we depleted our financial resources to support David, we had also turned all of our emotional energy toward keeping him sober. Our efforts had come to nothing.

We had already attended occasional Al-Anon meetings, but now we committed ourselves to regular attendance. I think it's not so much that misery loves company but that, during these meetings, the participants draw on the strength and experience of others who have suffered the impact of an addicted loved one. We heard numerous stories that were more dire than ours, and yet often the person sharing the story displayed the most impressive serenity—one of several powerful words that have come to represent the organization's philosophy. The message is simple: it's impossible to change the addict; you can only change yourself.

We were regularly advised that we must take care of ourselves by engaging in the things that gave us joy. When I first heard this, it struck me as impossible, shallow, and self-indulgent. How was I supposed to enjoy anything when my son was so desperately ill? Susan felt precisely the same. Wouldn't it be selfish to engage in things we loved? Shouldn't we focus all of our energy on David and his problems? We came to understand the wisdom of the advice, however, and were now determined to do everything in our power to take care of ourselves and to find ways to enjoy our lives, even in the face of our ongoing trauma. I had neglected my health and fitness and now took up a regular exercise program. Susan found friends with whom she played classical music and also joined a book club.

We also learned through our commitment to Al-Anon that the first step to regaining balance is acceptance. This is not to say that dealing with a loved one's addiction contains any joy—it doesn't. It is possible, however, not to identify with the problem. Curiously, detaching from the problem, but not the person who suffers from it, is the path to serenity. Through a tortured emotional journey, I came to accept that David was an addict and that I couldn't make him well again. Having suffered so much from his pain and struggles, I asked myself what was the worst thing that could happen to him. The answer: he could die at any time from his disease. Yes, he could die and would die if he continued to abuse alcohol and drugs. I had to accept this. After all, everybody dies. No parent wants to bury a child, but this happens. By accepting this worst possible outcome, I was able to gain some measure of serenity. I could love my son; I could hope that he would seek to regain his health; I would grieve if he didn't make it. But in the end, I alone was responsible for my serenity and equanimity.

In addition to taking care of myself, I was also determined to put to good use my experience, both as the father of an adolescent addict and as a Head of School, to craft an effective approach for my school—and hopefully others—to deal with student alcohol and drug use. I knew this wouldn't be an easy matter, but I also knew that this destructive behavior represented nothing short of a national crisis. I felt obligated to do everything in my power to ameliorate a scourge, and I was convinced that there was no Head of School more motivated or better prepared to tackle the problem. To be sure, my experience with my son forced the matter to my attention, but I understood that David's struggle was only one example of a problem that afflicted so many students all across the country.

As I considered the task ahead, I was mindful of the reaction to David's transgression and its aftermath. From the hateful and inaccurate anonymous letter, to allegations that I had forced teachers to home school my son, to the general pleasure that some people take in others' pain, the incident had brought out the worst in many elements of my school community. Too frequently, people resort to rumor and speculation in the absence of clear policies and behavioral norms; so this reaction was to be expected.

I understood that to be successful it would be necessary to build a policy and approach from the ground up. Ultimately, no policy or set of practices can be successful unless they're consistent with the culture and values of the school. I had been at pains in my leadership to foster an ethos of care and attention to every student. I believed it would be possible to apply these values to the way the school handled all aspects of student alcohol and drug use, including prevention, education, and discipline, as well as communication with families and support of the individual student.

With these basic goals in place, I convened a committee that included trustees, administrators, teachers, students, parents, and outside experts in the field of addiction. The committee was charged with writing a new policy to guide the school's response to student alcohol and drug use. The earlier policy was unclear and shrouded in myth and mystery. The prevailing myth was that the school maintained a "zero tolerance" policy on this issue. In fact, nowhere in any published literature, including the Parent/Student Handbook, was such language used. Rather, alcohol and drug use was listed among numerous behavioral infractions, both trivial and serious, that could result in disciplinary actions ranging from detention to expulsion.

Nonetheless, there was a widely held belief that alcohol or drug use would result in expulsion. This perception held sway even though my predecessor had exercised his discretion in determining the consequences for these offenses.

There *are* schools that maintain a "zero tolerance" policy, in the sense that there is a single sanction—expulsion—for those who offend. This approach grew out of "zero tolerance" in many public school systems for the possession of weapons on school grounds. While it's certainly possible to argue its merits, every reasonable person would agree that severe consequences are warranted when the physical safety of students is placed at risk by the presence of weapons. What is not at all clear is that a policy applied for weapons possession is appropriate in cases of alcohol and drug use.

The very term is misleading and damaging. Of course, schools maintain "zero tolerance" for alcohol and drug use. What school would tolerate such destructive behavior? The appropriate consequence for infractions is, however, another matter. Should every infraction, no matter the circumstances, result in expulsion? Many parents comfort themselves in the belief that if schools deal harshly with student offenders, their own children will be safe from the influence of bad apples. But there is no evidence that such policies serve as a deterrent to student experimentation with alcohol and drugs. National data from the 2012 Monitoring the Future survey reveal that 71.9% of 12th graders have tried alcohol, and 42% of them have tried marijuana. In the 30-day period prior to the survey, 65.5% of these students reported that they had consumed alcohol, and 32.4% reported smoking marijuana. The survey results are alarming: 40% of 12th graders, 31% of 10th graders, and 15% of 8th graders reported using one or more drugs in the past 12 months. While alcohol consumption has been declining for the past 20 years, the use of marijuana is steadily rising. The greatest concern is the high incidence of daily use: fully one in 15 high school seniors reported using marijuana at least 20 times in the 30 days prior to the survey.[3]

With such widespread use, schools simply cannot punish their way out of the problem. Instead, the challenge is to provide programs that aim at prevention and policies that at once discourage use and offer incentives to seek counseling and therapy for students who do use.

I've asked myself repeatedly how things might have been different in David's case had better programs and policies been in place at Brentwood School. Candidly, I don't think any programs would have prevented him from experimenting. I had been completely open with him about the impact of alcohol on my family, and Susan and I were very clear that we did not condone underage drinking. Yet like so many adolescents, he was determined to experiment. Unfortunately, he drew the short genetic straw and was predisposed to addiction.

Better, clearer policies, however, would have made a difference in the entire school community's response to his disciplinary outcome. They would have known how the process would be conducted and the rumor mill would not have been fueled. With a first offense, about which David was entirely truthful, he would likely not have been suspended for a semester, wouldn't have had his schooling interrupted, and wouldn't have suffered social isolation. Our family would have been spared the most hateful behaviors, and my leadership would have been far less compromised. As it was, the incident hurt David, our family, and the school. I was under no illusion that the work ahead would be easy, but I knew that the school had to have a more humane and sophisticated approach to student alcohol and drug use.

Our committee first sought to understand the causes and extent of alcohol and drug use at Brentwood. The students who served on the committee were invaluable resources for helping us understand the issues from the students' perspective; their insights would later be confirmed through extensive, anonymous surveying of the student body. They maintained that use was widespread and tended to increase as students passed from grade to grade. Most of the use occurred in the context of parties on Friday and Saturday evenings. The primary cause of the use was to relieve stress that resulted from pressure to succeed academically. They also stated that this academic pressure came primarily from parents and secondarily from the students themselves, because they had internalized the importance of success defined by earning good grades. They didn't believe that there was very much explicit pressure to use, but rather that the culture of use was so pervasive that many students felt they needed to use in order to fit in. This bleak analysis, coupled with one of the student member's assertion that nothing could be done about the problem, made clear that the committee's task would be daunting.

The first step was to draft a clear and effective policy, which was done after considering the views of the various committee members and reviewing the policies of a number of similar schools. It was then vetted by the school's legal counsel and presented to the Board of Trustees, which approved and adopted it, as follows:

Alcohol and Substance Abuse Policy

The Brentwood School community is concerned about alcohol and substance abuse among minors. The school expects that parents will not serve alcohol or other unlawful substances to students. Brentwood School encourages parents to contact the parents of their children's friends to discuss this most important issue.

Standards of Conduct: To carry out its educational mission and to foster the best learning environment for every student, the school strictly prohibits the following student behaviors on campus, at any offcampus Brentwood School-related event or activity, or anywhere the student acts as a representative of the school:

• The sale, distribution, possession, or use of tobacco, alcohol, illegal substances, or drug paraphernalia.

• Being under the influence of alcohol or any other illegal or mood-altering substance.

• The misuse of prescribed medication. Medication should not be administered other than in accordance with the labeled use as prescribed by a physician. Students should not administer their own prescription medication. It can only be administered by authorized school personnel.

Review Procedures: Any alleged infraction of the above standards of conduct should be reported to the student's Division Director. The Division Director will notify the student and the student's parents/guardians of the alleged infraction before the matter proceeds with a formal review.

• Lower Division: cases will be reviewed by the Division Director, the Assistant Director, the School Counselor, and the Nurse.

• Middle Division: cases will be reviewed by the Division Director, Dean of Students, and School Psychologist.

• Upper Division: cases will be reviewed by the Honor Board. After reviewing the case, the person(s) undertaking the review will submit recommendations to the Head of School. Depending upon the circumstances, recommendations may range from dismissal of the case to a student's expulsion from school. As in all disciplinary cases, the Head of School makes the final decision. If an infraction is determined to have occurred, at a minimum, the student will be placed on probation and may be required to agree to counseling, medical treatment, and/or ongoing drug testing as a condition of remaining enrolled in the school. Subsequent infractions are likely to result in expulsion from school but, at a minimum, will result in progressive discipline. Communication of all decisions will be at the discretion of the Head of School. When appropriate, the school will refer cases to the applicable federal, state, or local agencies.

Michael D. Pratt

Central to the policy was the certainty of consequences and the Head of School's discretion in determining the disciplinary response, which could range from mandated therapy to expulsion. I'm convinced that Heads of School must have this discretion in handling disciplinary matters. This is especially true in cases of alcohol and drug use, which involve both behavioral and health-related issues. Regarded solely from the behavioral perspective, the circumstances of the use should be considered in determining the consequence. What is the age of the student? How long has the student been in the school? Is the use a first or repeated offense? Did the use occur on school grounds or at a school-sponsored event? Is the offender merely a personal user or a seller? All of these questions are germane. The vital point is that while there must be consequences for use, the discipline should be balanced with support for the involved student and the family.

Beyond recommending the new policy, which provided clarity to the entire school community, the committee urged further study of the causes and extent of student use and the development of prevention programs. In fact, the school already had some prevention programs in place, but we knew these needed to be expanded and become more impactful. The first step was to gather data on use patterns and attitudes about use. To deepen our understanding, the school hired Freedom from Chemical Dependency (FCD), a nonprofit substance abuse prevention organization founded in 1976. FCD has served hundreds of schools and colleges in developing useful approaches to substance abuse prevention. Initially, they sent two representatives to interview members from every constituency in the school on their beliefs about student use of alcohol and drugs and how the school should handle the problem. The report suggested that the community believed that the problem was widespread and that the school should develop a consistent and sustained approach to dealing with it. The following anonymous quotes illustrate the school community's beliefs and confusion at the time.

• I guess I don't know what we're doing re: substance abuse, and maybe that is indicative of a problem…maybe not. I assume that we have and enforce a zero tolerance policy.

• The school has 0 tolerance. This is good.

• Launch a major P.R. campaign with parents to help reduce the amount of drinking at home parties.

• It seems to me that Brentwood's hard line on drug use on campus is appropriate. However, I think education on the danger of drug use is not ongoing enough. We need to integrate this teaching into the curriculum more.

• Use and abuse is probably _far_ _more_ widespread than Brentwood realizes. The policies we have in place to deal with these issues are good—I strongly urge that we never compromise our standards nor relax our vigilance.

Subsequently the school administered an FCD comprehensive, anonymous survey to students in grades 9-12 that compiled and analyzed data about individual student use, beliefs about other students' use, and perceptions about the reasons for use.

The data suggested that Brentwood School students' use patterns varied very little from national trends. Also consistent with national data, Brentwood students' beliefs about their peers' use grossly exaggerated actual use. The effect of this exaggeration is to normalize destructive behaviors. In other words, students come to believe that it's okay to drink and use drugs because "everybody" does.

The primary reason cited for use was parental pressure to earn good grades. In one of our family sessions with

Michael D. Pratt

David, he said he'd always felt under intense pressure to perform. We were shocked, because we rarely mentioned a word about grades. We didn't need to. With two Ph.D.'s for parents and one of them the Head of his school, he knew how highly we regarded education. His assertion did remind me that Susan and I had once teased him that he should get a Ph.D., so that his license plate could be DHP-PHD (his initials and his degree), the perfect palindrome. His response: "I don't want a Ph.D." Even in the absence of explicit reminders to work hard, students at schools such as Brentwood feel pressure. They understand that their parents pay the tuition with the expectation that there will be a pay-off in the end: matriculation at a "good college." David was no different: he felt pressure, even if we didn't tell him that he must earn good grades.

I frequently urged parents not to focus on grades, but rather on their student's interests, engagement, and effort, since emphasis on grades often diminishes the love of learning. It's not surprising that some students resort to using stimulants to gain an academic edge. With a growing number of students being diagnosed with ADHD and taking prescribed medications, these drugs are now widely available for purchase by other students. I knew that most parents would not heed my advice. The reality is that grades are the currency in schools such as Brentwood. Grades do matter, and students know this.

Some stress in life is inevitable and can be a positive, motivating force. Too much stress, however, is paralyzing. Ultimately, we came to believe that the school should undertake reforms to relieve unnecessary stress, to help students develop greater resilience, and to educate them about the true extent and health consequences of alcohol and drug use. Simple reforms such as no-homework weekends when students were expected to participate in school events, no extended classes during lunch, and clearly defined limits on the number of tests and major assignments due on any single day reduced academic pressure. To help students manage stress and become more resilient, the school also provided regular and ongoing sessions for yoga and mindfulness training. For the most part, the faculty embraced these reforms, and students and their parents were genuinely grateful. Interestingly, this more humane approach didn't diminish, but rather strengthened, student output and performance.

I have no doubt that these reforms had a positive impact on many students' experience, but of course alcohol and drug use didn't end. Equally important was how the school responded to reports that a student was using. Based on my own experience, I knew that most parents would appreciate knowing about their child's use, particularly if they could depend on the school to partner with them in getting help. After David had been busted for drug use, one of my trustees told me she'd heard he'd been partying heavily. If she'd told me this earlier, it might have reinforced the warning signs we'd been given. This in turn might have prompted Susan and me to intervene more strongly with David and might even have stopped his downward spiral.

With this in mind, I made a practice of meeting with parents of students whom I had good reason to believe were using. I always made clear that the meeting was not disciplinary, but rather out of concern for their child's health. In most cases, the parents were shocked and in denial. Just as with Susan and me, they trusted their child and asserted that they would know if their child was using. I would reiterate that I was not making an accusation, but rather was reporting a concern that I believed warranted careful consideration. For their peace of mind, I urged them to have their child tested. I then brought the student into the meeting and made the same report. Invariably, the student would deny using, but would realize there was no choice but to agree to be tested. More often than not, the test would come back positive for drug use.

I was gratified that parents eventually appreciated this intervention. The keys to success were that the communication was fully confidential, and there were no disciplinary consequences unless the behavior continued and occurred at school or a school-related event. Of course, these kinds of meetings are difficult, but the consequences of turning a blind eye on the problem until the student is caught are dire. Schools can and should develop humane approaches to what is a national health crisis.

Intervention

With a new policy in place at school, I felt deeply gratified. It provided clarity; more importantly, its general acceptance signified a culture shift. The community accepted that, as in every other school, some of our students used alcohol and drugs. Even though few would condone the use, virtually everyone understood that experimentation was endemic to adolescent culture, and the school needed enlightened policies and nuanced approaches to help students who found themselves in over their heads. Supported by this new attitude, I was able to help many students and their families in dealing with a devastating problem.

Our efforts to support our own son remained a challenge, one that often left us feeling defeated. By the summer of 2003, only a few months after graduating from Brentwood School, David was in his third rehab, this time at Journeys in Utah for an indefinite stay. Susan and I knew we couldn't allow ourselves to be discouraged, because negative emotions would harm all three of us. Nonetheless, our hopes had been dashed again and again, and we both experienced many dark moments.

Journeys, while having adequate amenities, was considerably less luxurious than Cirque Lodge, and the approach was much more direct and confrontational than David had previously experienced. Before Susan signed the paperwork for his admittance, we agreed she would tell him this was the last time we'd pay for rehab and that his sobriety would be up to him. When he responded that we didn't seem to have much confidence in him, Susan told him that the issue was actually about *his* confidence in himself.

Because family engagement is an important aspect of the recovery process, we planned to visit him periodically. When I went out to spend some time with him about a month later, I was convinced I saw small differences in his affect and attitude. He still held back in group sessions, but was very attentive and focused. When we had time alone, he said the director held him highly accountable, which David said was a good thing. He also talked about pursuing productive interests once he completed rehab. In general, he was more open and, at long last, willing to discuss the future. I left feeling more hopeful than I had in quite some time.

Susan and I returned to Utah to spend Thanksgiving with him. By this time, he'd moved from the main facility into a sober living home. He still attended group meetings and met with a counselor, but had more freedom, was permitted to look for a job, and had been hired to be a stock clerk in a retail store. We were pleased with this development—his first real employment. We both believed—and continue to do so—that more adolescents should work, as the experience deepens their sense of responsibility, makes them accountable to an authority other than their parents, and teaches them the fundamentals of money management. David spoke enthusiastically about earning some money and staying busy, and we took this as a very good sign.

Even though we saw much that was positive, we both came away concerned that something was wrong. Throughout the visit, he was pleasant and showed signs of sobriety and emerging maturity, but he was agitated. We didn't know precisely what this meant, but we'd seen the signs before. We knew better than to press him about his mood and attitude, because this generally meant he'd clam up. Our main concern always was to stay engaged and keep communication as open as possible. We also now realized that if there were a real problem, we'd learn soon enough. And we did.

At work, David was told never to climb on the shelves to place merchandise into high storage, but always to use a ladder. One day, he climbed on the shelves instead, was caught, reprimanded, and told he could lose his job. Which soon happened. He'd been at Journeys for about five months by this time, and the director had decided he should move on within a month. When David called to tell us he'd lost his job, we were on a short vacation, relaxing in Santa Barbara. Our first reaction was to go into the familiar downward emotional spiral, but we soon made a decision that there wasn't anything we could do about it, and that it was up to us to enjoy our time away together. Our Al-Anon training in detachment paid off.

We met for Christmas at David's grandparents' home in Colorado. The visit went well enough. He was cordial and polite—welcome changes from when he was using. Even so, he again seemed agitated and had difficulty staying engaged with the family. On the drive back to Utah, he seemed particularly taciturn and remote. When I decided to take a risk and asked him what the matter was, he responded that he always felt under intense pressure to appear to be doing well when he was with us. He sensed our emotional needs and tried to conform to our hope that he was sober and making steady progress in his recovery. The strain of being with the whole family had been difficult and wearing. Yet again, I was reminded of the value of the Al-Anon mantra: "Detach with love." The more we inquired, and the more solicitous we were, the more pressure and alienation he felt. When dealing with a child who's an addict, every natural instinct of a parent is confounded.

After consulting with close advisors, we agreed to move David to a sober living home in Northern California. When we dropped him off, Susan and I were both discouraged to discover a rundown facility in an undesirable area. All the residents were considerably older than he was, and several were paroled convicts. This was a far cry from his earlier experience, and we worried that he wouldn't be able to maintain his sobriety. To stay at the facility, he had to be sober; but there was very little structure. He was assigned no counselor, and was required to attend few meetings. He was also 18 and could leave whenever he chose.

He quickly found a retail job in Davis, a 13-mile commute from where he was staying. We thought the job was a good idea, as it would provide some structure and keep him accountable. However, commuting difficulties made him decide to leave the sober living home, and he began sharing an apartment with his work supervisor. We were concerned that he was no longer in a program to support his sobriety, but we thought living with his supervisor might keep him on the straight and narrow.

We drove up to visit and were pleased to see that their apartment was neat and clean, and glad when he told us he liked his job. We visited him at work, where he was doing very well and was an excellent employee. He knew the store merchandise and had excellent customer relations' skills.

We weren't surprised to find out that he'd established an impressive sales record. Within a matter of months, he was promoted to store manager at a different location. Susan and I were proud of his initiative and his willingness to put himself forward for a more responsible role. The downside of this very good news was that the new store was in Sacramento, a 25-mile commute. He'd have to get a car.

In a too-often-repeated pattern, I stepped in. Rather than leaving it to him to figure out, or even waiting for him to ask for help, I took the initiative to find him a relatively low-mileage car in excellent condition. He hadn't asked for my help; rather, I saw a problem, and fixed it. In hindsight, I realize I wasn't allowing David to develop important adult skills, but was sending a subtle message that I thought he was incompetent. The problem in this instance was that he had no savings and no credit record. Even though we had decided earlier that we would no longer accept financial responsibility for David, we couldn't see how he could purchase a car on his own. Reluctantly, Susan and I bought the car and set a schedule for him to repay us for the loan. For a while, all was well. With better pay in his managerial role, he had no trouble making the payments on time. Under his management, his store experienced improved sales, and he appeared to be flourishing. He enjoyed describing the changes he'd made in the store layout and the steps he'd taken to establish a more professional culture in the sales staff.

We were both looking forward to seeing it for ourselves. Since we were in Napa to spend Christmas with family, we drove over to Sacramento, arriving at the store at a particularly hectic time, as customers were flooding in to do their last-minute shopping. At closing, David had to reconcile the sales receipts for the day, and was very upset to discover they were off by almost $800. Frantically, he tried to figure out how the money could have gone missing. Before he was manager, the store had been robbed several times, so he thought a thief might have managed to grab money from the cash register while he or the other sales clerk was distracted. Later he discovered that he'd simply failed to record a deposit; but at the time he believed the money was missing and, whatever the reason, he'd be accountable. All three of us were anxious, and found it very difficult to enjoy the holiday gathering—I thought it likely that David would lose his job. This looked like just one more instance of a good opportunity turning sour.

After that time, it was difficult to make out how he was doing. He volunteered virtually no information about his personal life and only sporadically mentioned the store. We did learn that he'd had a minor fender-bender, and even though it was the other driver's fault, David hadn't followed up on collecting the insurance and getting the car repaired. Was he working his program, was he meeting with a sponsor—was he sober?

We soon got our answers. By late winter and into the spring, he became increasingly erratic in sending us his car payments. Initially they were late, and then were skipped altogether. He wasn't particularly skilled at handling money, but we were afraid he'd returned to using drugs, a very expensive habit. His sister Margaret soon confirmed our fears—David was again using heavily.

Although we now understood that relapse was typically part of recovery, we were demoralized. When would this end, and could it end well? So far, he'd been in three rehabs and a sober living home—to no avail. We could only think how different his life would have been had he avoided alcohol and drugs and attended college. And by now we'd already spent more on treatment than we would have on tuition.

We didn't know if another rehab would make any difference, but we certainly knew that the path he was on would end in death. We felt that rehab was the only viable option, but we also understood we couldn't force him to go, and that he'd have to figure out a way to pay for it himself. After much soul searching and discussion, we decided to stage an intervention and, at the same time, take away his car.

We knew David wouldn't welcome this kind of discussion, and certainly would try to wheedle his way into keeping the car; and I didn't know what I'd do if he refused to give me the keys. Though we didn't like deception, we believed that the intervention and taking the car couldn't be handled in a direct, transparent manner. Instead, we came up with a plan to take the car without his knowing, and tell him about it during the intervention.

Before moving ahead, we met with Jim Earnhardt to get his advice on how to proceed. We were as prepared as we could be for what we knew would be a very delicate situation; even so, we dreaded the confrontation. I called David about a week in advance to tell him I'd be in Sacramento the following weekend and wanted to take him out to dinner. I gave him a plausible reason for my being there, and he wasn't suspicious. I arranged a time for him to meet me in my hotel room, and asked him to call me on his cell when he arrived so I could give him my room number. Since I had no specific room assignment as yet, my request made sense. Of course, the real purpose was so that Susan and Margaret could then take his car using our extra key. Once they'd moved it to a different lot, they'd come to my room and we'd conduct the intervention. Until then, I'd ask David about his work and make small talk.

Everything went as planned, and he was naturally shocked when they arrived. I told him we were all together because we wanted to share with him how deeply concerned we were about the path he was on. The three of us in turn spoke from our hearts about our love for him and our hope that he'd return to rehab to regain his health and put his life back on course. Not surprisingly, he said he was fine and wouldn't go back, because he'd already gotten everything he needed there.

When it became clear that our pleas had fallen on deaf ears, I told him we'd taken the car, and asked him for his keys. I pointed out that he'd failed to make his payments to us as he'd promised and that, in any event, we wouldn't provide him with a car when we couldn't be confident he wouldn't drink and drive. He took the keys from his pocket and slid them across the table, while asking how he was supposed to get to work. We told him he'd have to figure that out for himself. In a response laced with expletives, he asked us to drop him off in Davis, and we agreed. Once we reached his neighborhood, he asked to be let out. I stopped the car, he got out, and we didn't know when or if we'd hear from him again.

Discharged

Eventually we did hear from him. The loss of the car meant he had to give up the managerial job in Sacramento and try to find another one back in Davis. Soon he began to complain about living with his former supervisor, describing him as immature and erratic. We later found out that he, too, experimented heavily with drugs. Fairly soon, David found a room in a large house that he rented with a number of other friends. On one of my visits, I was horrified to discover that his "room" was actually an unheated attic space, accessible only by an outside ladder attached to the side of the house. Just to go to the bathroom, he had to go back down the ladder. Even more worrisome, his room was filthy with "ashtrays" full of cigarette butts, dirty clothes strewn about, and stacks of beer cans and liquor bottles. I didn't know if he was still using drugs, but there was no doubt he was drinking heavily. He had a nasty gash on his head, which he said he'd gotten diving into a swimming pool. He'd obviously been drunk at the time. I tried not to look into the future, but the signs spelled trouble.

Like many alcoholics, David had developed an impressive range of coping skills and had managed to get reassigned to a store near Davis that he could reach via public transportation. He seemed to be back on an even keel, but we had no reason to assume he was sober, and by now we'd learned not to ask. He either was sober or not; and our wondering, worrying, and questioning made no difference. Though we periodically regressed in our understanding that David alone could bring about his sobriety, we mostly tried to stay engaged and accept what was.

Michael D. Pratt

In the summer of 2005, Susan came to visit him for his birthday, and David told her he was considering joining the armed services. A friend who'd been in the military suggested he meet with a recruitment officer. We supported this idea, because we respected service in the military as an honorable calling, and thought the discipline would be good for him. With wars in Iraq and Afghanistan, we worried what might happen, but we had grown used to worrying about his health and security. If he came to harm in the military, we rationalized, it would at least be in service to his country.

He ultimately decided to join the Navy, largely because it offered the best education and training that he could use when he reentered civilian life. He now faced the dilemma of how much he should disclose about his past to the recruitment officer. Ultimately, he stated he'd been in rehab for treatment for alcohol and substance abuse. The officer advised him to deny any use, but also said his tests had to be negative. When David said he wouldn't be able to pass right away, the officer said he could be tested informally and, once he did pass, could take the formal one.

I don't know if this practice was routine or officially sanctioned, but I think it's unconscionable to put a young adult in such a compromised position. Very few individuals old enough to join the military would have never consumed alcohol or used any drugs.

That a military official would advise him to lie in order to be inducted is an indication of the depth of misunderstanding of the nature of addiction, one that prevails not just in the military and schools, but in society in general. The belief persists that drinking and drug use are simple choices, and that users can just elect not to. If only it were that easy. I was troubled by the lie, but also hoped that the incentive to get sober might have positive consequences.

David finally cleared any trace of drugs from his system and became eligible for induction. Since his lease in Davis was set to expire a couple of months before that date, we agreed he should resign his job and return to Los Angeles to live with us in the meantime. We made it clear to him that he was welcome, but only on condition that he not use. Of course he agreed, as he had many times before. Things went well enough. He got a job and followed our house rules, as best we could tell. I was also impressed that he quit smoking and began exercising regularly to prepare for his physical testing and the rigors of boot camp.

Unlike earlier, we didn't remove the alcohol from our house, because we believed we should be able to carry on with our normal lives. But after a while, I began to notice that our wine and liquor supply was diminishing faster than I could account for. This prompted a search of David's room, which revealed empty bottles and a couple of partially consumed ones. More assurances and promises not kept. Susan and I found ourselves faced with a familiar dilemma: try to understand and give another chance, or hold him accountable and kick him out. We chose to allow him to stay in hopes that the Navy would prove to be a great opportunity and that he would break his physical dependence in boot camp.

At the same time, we knew we couldn't turn a blind eye to what he'd done. When we confronted him with the evidence and demanded an explanation, he apologized and said he hadn't been able to resist. I asked him how he planned to do so in the Navy, and he said he would have no choice in boot camp. Beyond that, he didn't know. Neither did we. I also asked him how much of our alcohol he'd consumed. Ultimately, we charged him for what he'd taken and again told him that his use wasn't acceptable.

This episode left me with several questions. Should we have invited him to return to Los Angeles to live with us prior to his induction, or left it to him to figure it out? Should we have gotten rid of all our liquor and wine before he moved back in? Should we have kicked him out after we discovered that he was drinking? None of these questions has an easy answer. Families who deal with alcoholism are often confounded. The most natural instincts to love, understand, and support are often rewarded with betrayal, disrespect, empty rationalizing, and even outright theft. Yet you know your child is struggling. You always hope that a bit of help at the right time will keep him moving forward, and you worry that the lack of it could send him over a cliff. That fall, the day arrived for David to leave for Sacramento, where he would undergo a wide range of testing to determine his physical and intellectual capabilities. He was found to be fit, tested extremely well, and shipped out to boot camp in Great Lakes, Illinois. I couldn't resist the hope that he would grow up under the demands of the military. In any event, he was now the Navy's problem, not ours.

We heard from him fairly regularly, and he appeared to be holding up quite well. He took a range of tests and, thanks to native ability and an excellent education, performed at a very high level. I took comfort in the belief that his alcohol and drug use hadn't diminished his intellectual capacity. He qualified for the Navy's nuclear propulsion program in Goose Creek, South Carolina; he'd chosen training that could be very useful once his term of service was complete. We attended his graduation ceremony and felt enormous pride and hope. He looked great, had succeeded at a high level, and appeared to have a bright future as a Machinist Mate. He would learn to maintain and repair the propulsion systems that powered nuclear ships and submarines. I was reminded of his interest in all things mechanical when he was a young boy. Once he and a friend retrieved a lawn mower from the garbage, brought it home, and began taking it apart with the intention of using the motor to propel a tank!

David was in a highly competitive program and was performing very well. The only glitch was that he needed a security clearance to move to the next level of training. Sailors in the nuclear propulsion program gain an intimate understanding of the mechanics of the propulsion systems, whose designs are classified, so the military has a strong interest in assuring that the information won't be leaked. Though he'd provided all of the requested information, weeks passed without a clearance.

I wondered at the time—and many times since—if the Navy's initial investigation revealed that he'd been in rehab. Since, on the advice of his recruitment officer, David had denied using, a question would have arisen as to why this was the case. I suspect that the Navy deliberately delayed the clearance process to see if he could maintain his sobriety.

We visited him during my school's spring break, three months into his deployment in South Carolina. We arrived at the base and, since we were not permitted to go to the building where he was staying, called him to arrange to meet in a nearby parking lot. As he approached, we barely recognized him. He had gained a fair amount of weight, which seemed odd since he had to meet fitness requirements. He said he'd continued to meet them, but that his training was highly sedentary and he wasn't getting much exercise.

He was excited to show us a recent purchase: a Kawasaki Ninja sport bike. He said it was an economical way to get around and was loads of fun. We resisted criticizing the purchase, but I felt strongly that it was a profligate expenditure. Why not save some money? For that matter, why not pay us back for the thousands of dollars we'd spent on rehab? Susan and I both regarded the motorcycle as relapse behavior; it felt like a new addiction, and we hoped he wouldn't combine this one with his others.

We had dinner together and enjoyed hearing all about his experience in South Carolina. He said the training was not terribly taxing and that he continued to perform near the top of his class. He liked being near Charleston and going into the city with his friends when he had time off. We agreed to meet at a restaurant there for breakfast the next morning, where one of my sisters and her family, who lived a couple of hours away, would join us.

David showed up with a serious limp. He said he'd twisted his ankle playing touch football with some friends on the base. I, of course, wondered if he'd been drunk at the time, but I'd learned not to say anything. We planned to walk around Old Charleston and go to other tourist attractions after breakfast. He managed to keep up despite obvious pain. Susan and I urged him to have it checked out, and he promised he would. Though the injury was initially diagnosed as a sprain, it proved to be the first of a number of broken bones he would sustain during the coming year.

Not long after that visit, he told us he'd been cited for speeding while driving his motorcycle on base. We later found out he'd also been cited for driving under the influence. He obviously hadn't endeared himself to the Navy brass. After all, the military actually expects service personnel to follow the rules.

The inevitable happened. Not long after the DUI, he told us he'd crashed his bike. I found myself wishing he'd totaled it, but no such luck, it was hardly damaged. David, however, had badly injured his left hand. Again, I wondered what the Navy made of this. In a matter of a few months, he'd broken an ankle, gotten a DUI on base, and broken his hand in a motorcycle crash. And there was still no clearance.

So there was plenty to worry about. He was drinking, and his behavior lacked what I thought of as "high seriousness." When I allowed myself to speculate on his future, I doubted he would make it in the Navy. Of course, I knew that agitating about this was of no help to me or to him. He certainly understood what was at stake. Trying to reason with him would be of no use; he alone would control his future.

He was in a period of limbo. The nuclear propulsion program included three levels of training. He'd completed the first with flying colors, but couldn't proceed until he was given clearance. Without the training structure, he spent a lot of time standing watch and doing tedious, menial tasks. Boredom had always been his enemy, and now that was frequently a factor. Before he was in a class for hours and had mandatory study periods, so there was little time for mischief. Without that structure, he had too much time on his hands and no sense of direction.

Around this same time, in the summer of 2006, his grandfather died, and David was given leave to attend the memorial service. As we were getting dressed beforehand, I noticed one of his arms was terribly bruised. I couldn't resist asking what had happened, and he explained that he and a friend had been playing "dead arm," a game in which contestants take turns punching the other in the arm until one gives up. This is not a game an adult—even a young male adult—plays unless drunk. At the gathering after the service, he drank heavily and, at one point, invited me to join him. Having just turned 21, he was now legally able to drink, but it was painful for me to watch, so I simply said: "I am not your drinking buddy."

In the past, David had experimented with a variety of drugs, but now that he was legally able to purchase alcohol, that had become his drug of choice. His appearance and his behavior made clear that he drank heavily and frequently. He was an alcoholic running headlong toward disaster.

Soon after he returned to South Carolina, David told us he had tested over the legal limit for alcohol. As if trying to lighten the blow, he said he thought he'd let enough time lapse between drinking and reporting for duty to pass the test. It was a clear example of the alcoholic mind at work; he continued to try to manage the drinking, even though he had an abundance of evidence that he couldn't. He hadn't yet made it to Step 1 in the Alcoholics Anonymous program—admitting that he was powerless over alcohol. I asked what the outcome would be. He said he was restricted to the base, would be fined, and would lose pay pending a final determination on his military status. Trying to prepare

Susan and me for the eventual outcome, he said it was likely he'd be discharged. Since this had happened to my Uncle Charles in the Army many years earlier, I wondered if the family history would repeat itself. Perhaps a week later, he called again to say this had happened. He turned down the Navy's offer to go into rehab for a month. His career was over in little more than a year, and what had started with so much promise ended abruptly with nothing but a motorcycle to show for the time. Later, when I asked if he knew he wouldn't make it through the program, he said he'd come to doubt he could stay sober. But this was apparently not an adequate wake-up call. What would it take?

Crash

In the days after David's discharge from the Navy, I grieved over another of his lost opportunities. Where would it end? His high school experience had been disrupted, he hadn't attended college, and he'd been discharged from the Navy. Again, I wondered where the bottom was for him, and how far he would have to fall before hitting it. I couldn't answer the question, so I had no choice but to fall back on an important Al-Anon mantra: "detach with love."

Over the next months, we had very little contact, and I was content to be in the dark about the details of his life. He made the choice to remain in South Carolina, where he got a job selling cell phones, rented a room, and carried on with his life. When we did speak, I asked generally how he was doing, but never pried and avoided giving advice.

The detachment, of course, didn't mean I wasn't worried. Since he'd refused the Navy's offer of rehab, I assumed he was still drinking, and just hoped that he didn't ride his motorcycle while under the influence. I wasn't worried he'd be arrested and lose his license—that would have been a blessing; rather, I was worried he'd kill himself.

I fell back on an old strategy to distract myself by becoming immersed in my work. Running a large, complex school provided me with innumerable opportunities, big and small, to focus on work rather than our family crisis. The school was engaged in developing an educational and facilities master plan that would be the blueprint for its future development. I was leading negotiations with the school's neighbors to adopt a conditional use permit to allow for the new facilities as well as growth in the student body. The project would come at a high cost, so I was also deeply involved in planning a large capital campaign.

At an annual event, a sports extravaganza against our archrival, I found myself standing beside Richard Rogg, the father of one of Brentwood's soccer players. This chance encounter would profoundly impact David's future. I'd met Richard a few times, but didn't know him very well, except that he owned Promises, a renowned alcohol and drug treatment center in Los Angeles. In part because of this connection, I assumed he must have known David's story, and was surprised when he asked if I had children. When I said that my son had graduated from Brentwood, and he asked where he was attending college, I decided to share a brief version of his troubles. (I started to think that my recent actions at school might actually have made a difference, since the rumor mill hadn't even reached Richard.) I explained that he'd become addicted to meth, never attended college, and was discharged from the Navy for alcohol abuse. Richard expressed his sorrow by saying, "Let me know if David ever needs a bed." I was profoundly touched by such generosity; but I expected nothing to come of the offer, since David had already gone the rehab route and was now rejecting every suggestion to return, whether it came from the Navy or his family. Events would soon transpire to change all of this.

****

The spring of 2007 was quite demanding. The school experienced an unusually high faculty turnover rate, so I had to devote a great deal of time to hiring. The workdays were long because there were numerous capital campaign donor thank-you dinners to attend. After one such event, Susan and I were particularly exhausted and were happy to return home and get to bed. I had barely fallen asleep when the phone rang. Foggy, nerves jangled, I fumbled for the receiver. I couldn't have anticipated the voice on the other end. "Dr. Pratt, it's Ahmad, David's friend from Menlo. I'm sorry to call at this time, but David's been in a really bad motorcycle crash. He's in the hospital, but I don't know his condition. I only know he wasn't wearing his helmet." The call I had feared had come.

When my breath came back and my throat loosened enough for me to speak, I asked Ahmad how he'd heard about the accident. He said that David's girlfriend had called him from the hospital because she didn't have our number. Since she wasn't a family member, she wasn't allowed to see him; and the emergency personnel would tell her nothing about his condition. I got her cell number, thanked Ahmad for contacting me, and hung up. Barely able to speak, I told Susan what had happened and went downstairs to call David's girlfriend to see if she'd found out anything more. I knew it would be an excruciatingly difficult call; we'd never met this young woman, and didn't even know of her existence. But I was aware that she was frantically trying to get information and was frightened about what she'd find out.

After quick introductions, she said she still hadn't heard anything specific from the medical staff; she only knew that a car had crossed in front of David and he'd broadsided it. He and the motorcycle flipped over the car, and the motorcycle had been destroyed. She could confirm that he wasn't wearing his helmet—which she couldn't understand, because he always wore it—and that he'd been taken to the hospital via medical helicopter. The conversation was terribly disjointed, but I was able to get her to focus on getting contact information so I could speak directly with someone knowledgeable about David's condition.

After what seemed an interminable delay, I finally reached an emergency room nurse who was assigned to David's case. She knew the basics: he had multiple fractures to his face, a skull fracture that resulted in a brain bleed of undetermined seriousness, a lacerated liver, a shattered left wrist, severe bruising from head to toe, and road rash.

She also said he'd likely survive, but it was too early to know if there was any permanent damage to his brain or spinal cord. She gave me a number to call in the morning for an update, when she thought a more definitive prognosis would be possible.

I went back upstairs to tell Susan everything I knew. My mind was swirling with conflicting thoughts. I had long expected such a call, but the belief that it would come was little preparation for when it actually did. I didn't know what I'd hear in the morning. Had he actually survived? Would there be brain damage? Would he be paralyzed? If he recovered, would this be the wake-up call that would lead to sobriety? Surely the crash would be his bottom.

And then, from nowhere, a horrible thought came into my mind: would it have been better if he'd died immediately from the crash? I chastised myself for thinking it, but there it was. Of course I loved my son and I didn't want him to die, but I had to wonder where his survival would lead. He'd thrown away one opportunity after another and was leading a dissolute life. He'd previously totaled a car and crashed his motorcycle. Would this far more serious crash just be another in a string of incidents until he killed himself or someone else? Feeling guilty about such thoughts was useless; I simply had to acknowledge that I could at once pray for my son's survival and worry where it might lead.

After a long, sleepless night, I called the hospital very early in the morning. The news was as good as I could have hoped. David had made it through the night, and his survival appeared to be secure. Neither the brain bleed nor the lacerated liver would require surgery. That said, he would face several surgeries to repair multiple fractures. His jaw was broken in two places and would have to be wired shut. Susan spoke later that day with the surgeon to grant permission to proceed, since David couldn't. In preparation for this, a tracheostomy tube had already been inserted to ensure an open airway. He was heavily sedated, so it was still impossible to know the extent of any neurological damage. I went to work while Susan made plans for us to fly to Charleston. Even though David's struggles were well known within the school community, I dreaded the prospect of having to share more bad news about him. I was certain everyone would assume he'd been drinking, and that the crash must have been his fault. I didn't want to discuss it, but I realized I'd have no choice.

The day was surreal. Susan and I spoke several times and decided to take a red-eye flight that evening. A Head of School can't simply disappear for an indefinite period, so I had to communicate fairly widely about what had happened. The inevitable avalanche of questions and expressions of concern immediately began. I knew the concerns were sincere, but I was so raw that I could hardly respond. After what seemed an eternity, I went home; we packed and headed for Charleston, not really knowing what to expect when we got there.

The next day, worn out from anxiety and travel, we finally arrived at the hospital and waited for a long time to meet with the physician overseeing our son's case. He assured us that David would recover and that early neurological tests looked promising. The left and right sides of his jaw were broken, so they'd inserted titanium plates to secure the bones in place while the fractures healed. His jaw was wired shut; once he was off intravenous feeding, he'd be on a liquid diet for six weeks until the wires could come off. (A perverse thought entered my mind: he'd already been on a liquid diet—alcohol—for months.) He was still in the surgical recovery room and we'd be able to see him when he was moved into the intensive care unit. Back in the waiting room, we met David's girlfriend for the first time and waited anxiously together to see him.

Wait. Wait. Wait. There's a lot of waiting in hospitals. Finally an intensive care nurse came and directed the three of us to his room. I fought back tears as I looked at my son;

if I hadn't known who was in the bed, I wouldn't have recognized him. Still unconscious, his head was terribly swollen, his protruding lower lip bruised and stitched, and his right eye was battered and strangely lower than the left eye. My handsome son was frighteningly disfigured. The nurse explained that he was still sedated but would be more alert shortly. We still didn't know if he'd sustained brain damage. Would he recognize us? Would he be able to communicate? Did he know what had happened or where he was? Our worst fears were soon put to rest—he knew us and tried to speak, but couldn't because of the wires holding his mouth shut. He made a writing gesture, so we got him a pen and paper and, in barely legible script, he asked what had happened. We explained about the crash, that he was in the hospital, and that he'd be okay. He nodded, paused, and scrawled: "I don't have insurance." I told him not to worry about that (though I certainly did). His left wrist was badly broken, but I assured him he'd still be able to play guitar. He then wrote a note to his girlfriend, telling her I also played guitar, but that he was a lot better. It was good to see he hadn't lost his sense of humor and playfulness. After a while, he drifted back to sleep and we left for the evening, knowing that the next day would be full of meetings with doctors and hospital administrators, contacting the police for an official accident report, and figuring out how to handle his recovery. Aware that we wouldn't be returning to Los Angeles any time soon, we both made arrangements to be away from work for an extended period.

The next day, we met with the doctor in charge of David's case to discuss the surgeries that lay ahead. The first order of business was to repair the orbital bone above his right eye. This fracture accounted for the swelling, bruising, and eye displacement. The doctor explained that the eyes had to be parallel or his vision would be impaired, and he couldn't guarantee that he'd ever recover complete vision. He also said there would be some scarring. Another surgery to repair the shattered left wrist would follow. Both procedures would require screwing titanium plates across the fractures to secure the bones while the breaks healed. Along with the metal plates already in his jaw, I figured David would in future set off airport security every time he flew. A nuisance perhaps, but a small price to pay to be back in one piece again.

We understood that follow-up procedures were necessary to remove the tracheostomy tube, the wiring from his jaw, and his wrist cast. Our more immediate concern, however, was the impending surgeries. We assumed that the hospital personnel were unaware that David was an alcoholic, and that this information might affect the kinds of pain management drugs that would be administered after the operation.

Narcotics of any kind wouldn't be good. When we let the doctor know about this complication, he expressed a new concern: since David wasn't getting alcohol in the hospital, and based on the level of his dependency, he might go through *delirium tremens (DTs)*. This possibility hadn't occurred to us, so we asked what the consequences might be. The doctor explained that *DTs* constituted a medical emergency associated with a high mortality rate if not treated early. I thought it ironic that he'd survived the motorcycle crash but could die from alcohol withdrawal. The doctor said that, in virtually every case, patients were disoriented, sometimes hallucinated, suffered paranoia, and occasionally required restraints to control autonomic manifestations, or involuntary muscle spasms. We said that our son had shown no signs of *DTs* so far, but the doctor said it wasn't unusual for the reaction to be delayed. There was nothing for us to do except wait and hope.

Later that day, we met with hospital administrators to review financial obligations. Given the level of care required, we knew they'd be exorbitant. Because he wasn't a college student, he couldn't be covered by our insurance; and we knew he had none of his own. He was 21 and wasn't our financial responsibility, but obviously he wasn't going to be able to pay the bills himself. We were left to hope that the insurance of the driver who had caused the crash would cover them. If not, the burden would fall to taxpayers.

There was nothing we could do to affect our son's medical condition except be there with him for support. On the other hand, we could try to find out as much as possible about the circumstances of his crash and about the driver who'd caused it. We contacted the police, were able to obtain the official accident report, and discovered that the young woman driver and a young male passenger were driving south along a two-lane road. At approximately 11:00 p.m., she'd made a left turn across David's path. Did she lose his headlight in the lights of the car behind him? Was she distracted by her passenger or something else in the car? Was she unfamiliar with the road or the car, which the accident report indicated didn't belong to her? We'll never know. In any event, he had no opportunity to avoid her. The motorcycle struck the front fender of the passenger side of the car, and David and the motorcycle catapulted over it and landed on the opposite side of the road.

Given the circumstances of the crash, I continue to believe that it's a miracle he survived. The speed limit on that stretch of highway was 45 miles per hour; he broadsided the car, and wasn't wearing a helmet. Later, when he was more fully aware of the event, he said he was sure he was driving faster than the speed limit, because he always rode aggressively. His pattern of injuries suggested that he contacted the road first with his left hand, and then with the right side of his forehead. He certainly flipped many times, accounting for the severe bruising on his legs.

We decided we might be able to gather some useful information at the accident scene. The mangled motorcycle and some of David's clothing had been removed, but parts of the bike, none bigger than a 50-cent piece, were scattered along the roadside. I contacted the local impounding facility, and the receptionist confirmed from the case number that they had what was left of the motorcycle. When I asked if I could come to see it and also pick up David's things, there was a long pause; then she said I could get his things, but the company advised against viewing the motorcycle because it would be "too hard for the family." I believe she assumed from the bike's condition that our son was dead. I told her I understood and would be by later to collect what was left: a blood-splattered motorcycle jacket and a pair of tennis shoes. That was it.

Why had he survived? I could resort to physics and imagine that he had flipped and landed in a particular way that prevented deadly trauma to his vital organs. And maybe it's as simple as that. On the other hand, he was wearing no helmet, and the remaining bits of the motorcycle were more than 60 feet from where he hit the car. I'm not a conventionally religious person, but I thought at the time, and continue to believe, that his survival was not mere happenstance. I don't begin to understand why he lived, but I'm convinced he was given another chance for a reason.

Realizing that this case was too complicated for us to handle on our own, we retained legal counsel to help navigate liability for the accident. We contacted a highly regarded Charleston attorney whose practice in part dealt with personal injury. I met him at the hospital, and he wasted no time in managing my expectations. In our initial conversation, I had outlined what I knew about the case and gave him the information from the police report. After expressing sympathy for what our family had suffered and reminding me that the important thing was that our son was alive, he said, in quintessentially southern fashion, "You can't get blood from a turnip." In short, we shouldn't expect to recover damages from the driver who caused the accident. I worried that David would be stuck with medical bills he could never repay resulting from an accident that wasn't his fault. And this is just what happened. The at-fault driver was uninsured, was driving a car that didn't belong to her, and disappeared after the crash. The attorney concluded there was simply nothing to be gained from pursuing the case. Appallingly unjust, but our son was alive.

I've wondered repeatedly since the crash if that driver is haunted by the experience. She felt the impact of the motorcycle, saw medical personnel arrive and David being evacuated by helicopter, was cited as being at fault by the investigating police, and then disappeared. David remembers nothing of the accident. What does she remember?

Back to waiting in the hospital room. Hours had turned into days, and I was beginning to understand why crossword puzzles and Sudoku were invented. Information from the surgeons and nurses was sparse. David had now completed his first round of surgeries—one to repair two breaks in his jaw, another to his right orbital bone, and a third on his wrist. He would have to remain in the hospital until he gained sufficient strength and balance to stand and walk, which would enable him to move around on his own and manage his recovery.

It was difficult for us to imagine that he'd be released any time soon, even though we understood that hospital beds come at a premium. We were relieved that my sister Tina, a nurse, was driving down from North Carolina for a short visit. We figured she could assess his condition and advise us on what we should ask the doctors. She had barely arrived before saying that David needed more attention and began directing his nurses. She said he was "disgusting" and gave him a bath. He soon looked and smelled considerably better. She had to leave after a few hours, and we were left to hope that we could manage David's continued recovery.

Even before she left, we had begun to notice subtle changes in David's interactions with those around him. Soon he became agitated, disoriented, and started pulling at his tracheostomy tube, which kept an open breathing passage. I tried to tell him not to touch it and, when he continued, I restrained his arms. Clearly hallucinating, he muttered through teeth clenched shut by wires, "Who the hell do you think you are coming in here and trying to manhandle me?" I knew he wasn't speaking rationally, but it broke my heart that he thought I was trying to harm him. It was the beginning of the *DTs*, and it was going to be a long night. We called for a nurse and explained what was happening. She administered Ativan, a benzodiazepine, to mitigate the effects of alcohol withdrawal, and called for an aide to apply restraints to his arms so that he couldn't injure himself.

The drugs helped calm him a bit, but he continued to hallucinate. He talked about having trouble cranking his motorcycle, and how some soldiers had helped him jump-start it. He asked for a cigarette. When I explained he was in a hospital and smoking wasn't allowed, he suggested we go outside. In vain, I explained that his injuries made it impossible for him to leave his bed; he was furious, arguing that the only problem was my refusing to help. Eventually the Ativan calmed him, and he fell into a restless sleep. The nurse said that his *DTs* were fairly typical for alcoholics and that he would be okay. We had no choice but to trust this was the case.

Once he was sleeping soundly, we left for the night; and it was a terribly long one. We'd been in Charleston for six days and were emotionally exhausted. If he survived that night's *DTs*, we didn't know how he'd be the following day. Neither of us was able to eat or sleep.

The next morning, still exhausted, we dragged ourselves into the hospital for more of the same. David was extremely agitated and belligerent. He began violently kicking the footboard of the bed and cursing like the proverbial sailor. He'd been discharged from the Navy, but he hadn't forgotten the lingo. We called for a nurse, who called for an aide, who calmly explained to him that, if he continued to kick, his legs would also be restrained. I don't know whether it was that threat or the effects of more medication, but he began to calm down.

Michael D. Pratt

Throughout the rest of the morning and into the afternoon, he mostly slept. When awake, he was increasingly calm; by evening, the *DTs* had ceased. He'd made it through this crisis, and the plan was to get him up on his feet the next day. We were deeply relieved and hopeful that he'd turned the corner in his recovery.

We now tried to focus on his long-term care. We knew he'd have to come back to Los Angeles with us. He had no transportation and wouldn't even be able to get to the hospital for follow-up visits; and with no insurance, he wouldn't be able to pay for any further care, even if he could get to the hospital. He also couldn't work for the foreseeable future, and so wouldn't be able to pay his rent. He wouldn't get treatment, and we were certain he'd start drinking again. Of the many times we'd faced difficult choices in trying to help David, this was the starkest. If we left him in Charleston, he would die. We saw no alternative; he would have to return with us to Los Angeles until his condition improved enough for him to live independently.

Despite our understanding of all these factors, we also worried that this involvement was a slippery slope, and that we could lose all we'd gained through Al-Anon. This is the classic dilemma when dealing with a loved one who's an addict. The natural instinct is to help, but when does that create a safety net that prevents the addict from hitting bottom and concluding that sobriety is the only way forward? And when does the help create a co-dependency that damages the helper?

Susan and I went to his rented room to gather his belongings, and saw evidence of a dissipated existence. Everything was in disarray, with cigarette butts and ashes everywhere, clothes and paperback books strewn about, and an almost-full bottle of cheap vodka. This is what his life had come to: get off from work at a dead-end job, go home, and retreat to his room to drink. Would this ever change?

We tried to figure out what was worth taking back with us. We set aside a lot of clothes to be taken to Goodwill. We threw out the vodka and the other empty bottles; packed the clothes worth keeping and loaded them, along with his guitar and amp, into the car; and cleaned his room as best we could. Ultimately, the amp was too heavy and bulky to ship, so we sold it to a music store at a cut rate.

Back at the hospital, David had finally turned a corner. The catheter had been removed, and he was able to get out of bed to go to the bathroom on his own. The more he was up, the more strength he gained, and the better he was able to breathe. He was eager to be up, so with my assistance we walked the hospital hallways together. Once off sedatives, he could think more clearly so Susan and I talked with him about our decision to bring him back home with us. I don't think he was thrilled, but he understood the necessity.

He was released after 12 days in the hospital. Before leaving, he was given a final check-up, and had the tracheostomy tube removed—leaving an open slit in his neck. He was given instructions on cleaning his various wounds and the trachea opening, and was told that, until this healed, he'd be able to talk more easily if he placed his fingers over the opening (not that he would do much talking with his jaw wired shut). He was also given a pair of wire cutters. The doctor explained that they must always be close by since, if he vomited, he could suffocate. We took him to our hotel room for a shower; bought him some shoes, pants, and a shirt for the trip back home; then to a barbershop for a haircut. The barber took one look at David and asked: "What's the other guy look like?" To us, given what he'd been through, he looked surprisingly good. Another night in the hotel, and then we were off to the airport and the flight back to Los Angeles. I didn't allow myself to think about the future.

Bottom

We were clear with David that he could stay with us for as long as his recovery required, but if he drank, he was out. We had to arrange his after-care, which included having the wires removed from his jaw and another surgery on his wrist. Without insurance, we knew that we'd be on the hook. Even though both procedures were done on an outpatient basis, and we'd negotiated the best possible rate, we still had to borrow from our retirement to pay the bill.

With the wires off, David was able to eat solid food for the first time in weeks. He was told not to overdo it in order to avoid potentially re-breaking his jaw. I was less worried about that than about his possible return to drinking. He'd stuck very close by during his recovery; but with the opening in his neck healed, the wires off his jaw, and the cast removed from his wrist, he now had more independence.

He'd also recovered remarkably well from the physical trauma of the crash. A small mark on his neck, a scar on his wrist, and his right eye open slightly wider than the left from the scar tissue were the only visible signs that anything had happened. Although he looked good and claimed to feel fine, we suspected there might be lingering psychological consequences from the discharge from the Navy, the crash, and leaving his girlfriend behind in the sudden departure from South Carolina. His life had undergone massive transitions, none of them positive. We urged him to meet with a therapist to process the recent past. We felt this would help him regain emotional balance and begin to take steps to rebuild his life. Very much to our surprise, he agreed, so we scheduled a next-day appointment.

Michael D. Pratt

The same evening we talked about his returning to therapy, he told us he was going out with a couple of his high school friends who were home from college for the summer. We decided not to say anything about drinking, but did tell him to check in with us when he got home. We'd been clear about our terms for his staying, and were determined to enforce those rules by testing him every time he went out. We were already in bed when he got back, but he came in as promised. I'd set a breath tester on my nightstand and told him to use it. He did, saying, "I won't pass." When I stupidly asked why, he said, "Because I drank." He was right; he didn't pass. I told him we'd talk about it in the morning.

Back to square one. We were distraught, but resolute—especially Susan—and we still thought it made sense for him to see the therapist. The next morning, even after showering, he still reeked of alcohol. He was making up for lost time. While he was at his appointment, we called Jim Earnhardt, who urged us to get David back into rehab. We said we were certain he'd resist and, in any event, we simply could not, would not spend another penny on rehab for an unwilling patient. Jim offered to try to convince David to go into rehab at Promises' West L.A. facility, and later met us at the therapist's office.

As we predicted, David was highly resistant. Jim could do no more than urge him to take a look at the facility and remind him that he was now an adult and didn't have to stay if he didn't like it. David said he'd think about it.

Back in the car, he said he really didn't even want to see the facility and just wanted to go home. Fortunately, Susan's resolve was stronger than mine; she said he could go home just long enough to gather his few things and leave. When he belligerently asked how he was supposed to do that with no transportation, Susan told him he'd just have to figure that out for himself. He then asked if he could have some time to make a few calls to arrange to leave. Susan responded without hesitation. "Your choices are to go into rehab or go home, gather your things, and leave immediately." David said that, since we were leaving him no choice, he'd take a look at Promises. Susan reminded him that he *did* have a choice: rehab or the street. Alcoholics require stark choices.

Jim had already spoken with Betty Wyman and Richard Rogg, the Brentwood parent I'd met earlier in the year, who was willing to take David in at Promises. Susan and I were profoundly grateful for this generosity, but we didn't know if he'd have the good sense to grab hold of the lifeline. To our great relief, he agreed to stay. Since this put a roof over his head and food in his mouth, we thought it likely he'd stay for the entire 30 days.

We didn't know if that amount of time would make a difference, but we were relieved that he'd at least be safe for a month. As in previous rehabs, we were encouraged to take an active role in the recovery process. We committed ourselves to attending sessions with the other families and met individually with David and his counselor. In these sessions, for the first time, he showed how strongly he resented our trying to control him and how we were imposing expectations that he didn't share. He claimed not to care about going to college, and said he enjoyed his life. We understood this was the alcoholic mind at work, but it was difficult to listen and respond without defensiveness and anger. In reality, we felt we should have demanded more from him and been explicit about those expectations. His counselor reminded us privately that this was the alcoholic speaking, and that his opening up was actually a good thing. We were left to hope that this was a breakthrough, even if it was hard to take.

The counseling sessions became increasingly productive, and David appeared more settled and focused. Happily, he no longer indulged in blaming us for his problems and was candid about his feelings. At the end of the month, he moved into a sober living home, which gave him a great deal more freedom. We met with him regularly, took him shopping, and occasionally went out to dinner.

We also attended Promises' meetings for the loved ones of alcoholics. Even though based on 12-step program principles, their meetings aren't formally affiliated with Al-Anon, where participants typically share their experiences but don't respond to each other in "cross-talk." At Promises, the facilitators and the other participants often challenged assumptions and gave advice. This particular group was a godsend to us, and we continued to attend until we moved from Los Angeles four years later.

At one meeting, which took place while David was in the sober living home, the father of another Promises patient asked us what we thought of our son's new motorcycle. I asked, "What motorcycle?" He replied, "Oh, I thought you knew."

Once again, Susan and I saw this new purchase as relapse behavior. It wasn't alcohol, but it was a severe lapse of judgment. I'd already planned to meet with him the next day for lunch, so I asked him matter-of-factly about it and why he hadn't told us. He said he'd intended to, but just hadn't gotten around to it. I asked how he'd paid for it, and he said he'd taken out a loan; I found it incredible he could have gotten one. I was clear with him what Susan and I thought about the purchase. He'd nearly been killed in a motorcycle crash, had daunting medical expenses, and no job. He assured me he'd get work and that the motorcycle was economical transportation. I'd heard this before; I knew this was the alcoholic speaking. He owed us thousands of dollars and had no enthusiasm or energy for adult responsibilities, but somehow found the initiative to purchase another motorcycle. Susan and I were furious.

Within a week of hearing about this, we got a devastating call from David's sober living counselor, who said that a search of David's room had turned up a bottle of liquor. The rules were clear: he couldn't remain in the home if he drank. The counselor offered him one more chance, but

David was unwilling to stop drinking and left on his motorcycle without saying where he planned to go.

We were worried sick about him, but knew it was best to let him contact us when he was ready. We thought he might have reconnected with some of his friends from Davis, whom we didn't know, or perhaps his Menlo School friend, Ahmad; so we called to see if he'd heard anything. He told us that David, obviously drunk, had called to ask if he could stay with him for a while. Ahmad had told him he could come for a day or two, but that he couldn't move in unless he was committed to sobriety. He never showed up, so Ahmad didn't know where he was now. We were enormously grateful to Ahmad for being firm and clear with David because, as long as he had a safety net, he'd never get sober.

We again had no choice but to hope that he was safe and wait to hear from him. A couple of mornings later, while I was at school, my assistant interrupted a meeting to say that Susan was on the phone and needed to speak to me right away. Since she'd never done anything like this before, I was terribly worried. What I heard took my breath away: Richard Rogg had called; David had contacted him to ask if he could come back to Promises. He'd hit bottom and was ready to get sober for himself.

Epilogue

David had hit bottom. When I comprehended the significance of his decision to return to Promises on his own accord, I was full of hope, but not expectations. We had lived through this cycle so many times, only to have our hopes dashed. I could feel myself guarding against looking beyond the next day. Was this really his bottom, and did this really mean he was ready to get sober? He'd already lost so much; why was this time any different?

In fact, it's impossible to know what any individual's bottom is. In some cases, perhaps it's a single crushing experience; in others, it might be the accumulation of consequences. All David could say, well after the fact, is that, having found himself thoroughly drunk in a cheap motel in East Los Angeles, he couldn't answer a simple question that he posed to himself: "What's next?" Having blown so many opportunities and lost so much, he no longer had a vision for his life. With no sense of any way forward, he understood that sobriety was his only and final option.

Even though he'd voluntarily returned to rehab fully independent of our desires or demands, he was still profoundly angry with us and initially refused to see us. We were well beyond being hurt by his actions and simply hoped that this rejection was a necessary step in his recovery. Over time, he re-engaged and admitted that the real issue was that he was embarrassed. How many times could he let us—and himself—down? Initially, it was easier to be angry with us rather than reflect on his own shortcomings. Eventually, we attended the family sessions and were able to support him in his recovery.

During this stay in rehab, David received an experimental pharmaceutical treatment, a series of three injections of Prometa, a combination of three drugs that have been used individually for some time to treat other conditions and which, in some cases, reduces the patient's cravings. Prometa and other drugs, such as Vigabatrin, a gama vinyl-GABA or GVG, hold out promise that alcoholism and addiction might be successfully treated, thus mitigating the destruction this disease wreaks on countless lives. A pharmaceutical treatment might also once and for all make clear that alcoholism and addiction are diseases of the brain and not the product of willfulness or the lack of willpower.

Like many patients who receive Prometa, David claimed that he didn't feel any different after the treatment, but we noticed some changes. He was more focused, less agitated, and more deliberate in his approach to treatment. After five weeks, it was time for him to leave rehab; for the first time in a very long while, we thought he might maintain his sobriety.

Today, David is healthy, employed, and a father. When he speaks about alcohol and drugs, he says simply that they are not an option for him. He knows he's not cured, but is only in recovery. Having slipped in the past, he knows it could happen again unless he's constantly vigilant.

In the darkest days of David's addiction, we didn't know if he would make it. Through his own desire to live, boundaries that we set in our relationship with him, the kindness and generosity of key individuals, and gifted and committed therapists, we have our son back.

When I became Brentwood's Head of School, I was ambitious to make a difference. I had envisioned building innovative programs for students and teachers, strengthening fundraising, improving the school's admissions profile, and helping seniors compete for spots in the top colleges. All of those things happened. It never once occurred to me, however, that I would be called upon to devote so much time and energy to developing a more humane and balanced approach to student alcohol and drug use. David's illness was a terrible struggle—for him and for our entire family. But as I look back on it, I know that the school community benefitted from our pain.

It's rare in life that we get to plan what we're called to do. After having the privilege of serving as Head at Brentwood School for 10 years, I left with the satisfaction of having accomplished most of what I had intended. Yet it's what I had not planned that is perhaps my most important legacy. I never imagined that my son's experimentation with alcohol and drugs, and his subsequent addiction, would force me to take on a serious social ill. Yes, David's struggle was a family crisis; but it was one that afflicts so many other families. In this case, it was impossible to separate the personal from the professional. In coming to understand my son's disease, I was better able to support him and to make a difference in the lives of many other students and their families.

Advice to Parents

Parents are right to worry that their children will experiment with alcohol and drugs. National data on adolescent use confirm widespread experimentation, and that it's beginning earlier and earlier.

The use of alcohol and drugs happens frequently in social settings that place adolescents at high risk, and we know that using impairs judgment—something adolescents can ill afford. In these circumstances, they are far more likely to engage in dangerous behaviors, including sex, driving while under the influence, or riding with others who are driving under the influence.

Some estimates suggest that up to 10% of the population is genetically predisposed to addiction, and that dependence and addiction are more likely the earlier the use begins. Children who drink by the time they're 15 are 40-60% more likely than the rest of the population to develop alcoholism in later life. Adolescents who abuse alcohol and drugs frequently and chronically face these risks, but also typically perform poorly in school, become estranged from their families, and lose many of their friends.

It's essential that parents be aware of the risks associated with experimenting with alcohol and drugs, take steps to prevent it, and be alert to signs that their child is using. Even though no parent can be assured that his or her child will abstain, there are ways to reduce the likelihood of use and to intervene early once use has begun.

Michael D. Pratt

Practical Advice to Prevent or Postpone Use

• Learn the difference between abuse and addiction, and between behavior and disease.

• Remember that your children are watching you, so don't use controlled substances or abuse alcohol or prescription medications. This doesn't mean that you can't drink responsibly. It does mean that your children will notice if you abuse alcohol or drugs; and, if you do, your children are likely to imitate this destructive behavior.

• Be explicit and clear about your values. Evidence indicates that children are less likely to use when their parents have discussed their expectations openly and often.

• Provide your children with accurate information about the legal, health, educational, and social risks of use.

• Do not serve alcohol to your minor children, even on holidays and at family ceremonies. This is a controversial position, because some parents believe they should teach their children how to drink responsibly. Many believe their children will drink anyway, and that it's better that they do it at home rather than in an uncontrolled setting with their peers. But it's actually better that they don't drink in either setting. It's certain that if children are permitted to drink at home, they'll drink with their peers. It's also clear, as the estimates mentioned previously show, that the longer drinking can be delayed, the better. Parents should never condone underage drinking.

• Never, never, never serve alcohol to your children and their peers in any setting. To put it bluntly, serving alcohol to minors is illegal and sends the clear message that such activity is fine.

Signs Your Child is Using

Owing to a neural pruning process in the brain and raging hormones that occur during adolescence, your child's behavior will appear bizarre from time to time, even in the absence of alcohol or drug use. It's also normal for children to spend more time with their peers and to get their sense of identity from them, not their parents. This process is perfectly normal and necessary, but it can be painful and unnerving for parents. All of these factors make it difficult to know with certainty that your child is using. Even so, there are signs that you should recognize.

Physical Signs

• Red and/or watery eyes. This condition can indicate the use of a variety of drugs.

• Unusual or sudden onset of lethargy.

• Inability to sleep at night. Many adolescents experience changing sleep patterns, but chronic inability to sleep at night can indicate the use of stimulants.

• Smell of alcohol or smoke on breath or clothing. Parents should be especially alert to the smell of tobacco, which is harmful and powerfully addictive, and is often the beginning of more serious drug use.

• Rapid weight loss. Many teens, especially girls, experience weight fluctuations; but rapid weight loss can indicate the use of cocaine or other stimulants.

Michael D. Pratt

• Sudden and aggressive onset of acne. Adolescents are notoriously susceptible to this skin condition; but when a severe outbreak coincides with insomnia, it could be a sign that your child is experimenting with methamphetamine.

Behavioral Signs

• Excessive and chronic moodiness or agitation.

• Excessive argumentativeness. Yes, adolescents are argumentative; but if the incidence and vehemence increase, this could indicate drug use.

• Loss of initiative. Alcohol and drug use diminish initiative. Parents should be aware of their child's loss of interest in school and activities that were formerly enjoyable. When students experiment with alcohol and drugs, their academic performance often suffers significantly.

• Secretiveness. Rarely do adolescents believe that their parents would approve of their alcohol or drug use, so naturally they seek to conceal any such activity. Adolescents typically communicate less with their parents, but if the communication seems deceptive, parents should consider the possibility that their child is hiding alcohol and/or drug use.

Social Signs

• Sudden change of friends. Adolescents who don't use alcohol and drugs typically don't want to be around those who do. Users, like all adolescents, are also painfully eager to be accepted by their peers, so tend to navigate to groups where approval is likely. Unfortunately, the price of admission to social groups that drink and use drugs is low: open mouth, ingest.

• Isolation. Excessive use of alcohol and drugs often causes adolescents to lose their friends. In severe cases of abuse, the user becomes isolated and uses alone.

What Parents Should Do If They Know or Suspect Their Child Is Using

Few things are as distressing to parents as discovering that their children are using, and with good reason, because the stakes are so high. Some parents might dismiss their concerns in the misguided belief that all adolescents experiment at some point, and that this is a temporary phase that their child will grow out of. In fact, this attitude places a child at very high risk for developing alcohol or drug abuse and dependence. Parents should work very hard to prevent or postpone their child's experimentation. The following are practical steps parents can take if they observe signs that their child is using:

• Confront firmly but without anger. It's essential to reaffirm that use is not acceptable. The typical adolescent response is to react defensively and deny use.

• Set up a regimen of random testing. Your child will almost certainly be angry with you for your lack of trust. A useful response is that the testing is a way to re-establish trust and, if the tests are clean, there's nothing to be concerned about.

• If the testing or other observation confirms use, arrange for counseling. Frequently, adolescents use for underlying psychological reasons. Effective treatment of the cause can end or significantly diminish use.

Michael D. Pratt

• If the use has progressed to abuse and dependence, a counselor with special expertise in substance abuse should augment or replace traditional counseling. The drug counselor may recommend that the parents and child develop a contract that sets out behavioral expectations that must be met in order for the adolescent to enjoy social freedoms.

• If the use continues or worsens, parents should consider placing their child in outpatient care. In this environment, the adolescent must be present at a treatment center when they're not at home or in school. In addition to individual counseling, outpatient care includes group sessions, frequent 12-step meetings, and sober social outings with the group. At some centers, there are tutors and structured study times to prevent the patient from falling behind in school.

• If addiction has developed, consider inpatient rehabilitation. These programs are very expensive and too frequently not covered by insurance. That said, inpatient rehab provides intensive counseling in a safe, highly structured environment.

The simple reality is that parents cannot prevent their children from experimenting, but they can take actions that significantly lessen the likelihood and potentially severe consequences. The investment is invaluable in the health and success of adolescents.

Advice to Schools

Few problems in schools are as pervasive or vexing as student alcohol and drug use. By the time they graduate from high school, almost 80% will have experimented, and an alarming number use regularly. This endangers student health and diminishes academic productivity and success. Anyone who has worked in schools knows that students learn in a social and emotional context, thus it is in a school's best interest to foster a healthy student body and school culture. Even so, surprisingly few schools have deliberately and thoughtfully sought solutions.

Traditionally, schools have pursued one of two courses. They have denied they have a problem and have swept individual transgressions under the carpet, or they embrace a "zero tolerance" policy and expel the offending student. In the first instance, the problem festers and the students become cynical. In the second, the education of the student who is caught is disrupted, and the student's family is thrown into chaos. Worse yet, the "zero tolerance" response doesn't deter other students from experimenting. Instead, it creates a culture of fear and silence.

The problem is real and there are no simple solutions. The stakes are high, and I believe that schools have a moral obligation to grapple thoughtfully with the problem. Based on my experience as a Head of School, I believe that success depends on a sustained, multifaceted approach that combines prevention education; effective counseling; policies that are clear, consistently applied, and communicated openly; and a culture that places a higher value on student wellness than on punishment. No matter how thoughtful the approach, some students will still experiment, and some will become addicted. The point of thoughtful approaches is to reduce the number who use and ameliorate the damage to the user and the school community. Consistent application of the following can make a difference:

School Culture

Progress depends on an acceptance that students will make mistakes and that they should be given an opportunity to redeem themselves. I believe that the purpose of a school is to educate, not to punish. We all know that much of the best learning is the result of making mistakes. Students who are caught using should absolutely be held accountable, because this teaches that actions have consequences, but overly harsh punishments unfortunately teach the wrong lessons. Building a school culture in which students are given the opportunity to learn from behavioral mistakes that don't harm others requires developing a consensus among all the constituencies within the school community. Just as it's important for students to learn from academic mistakes, so they should be given the opportunity to learn from behavioral ones.

A very positive consequence of a school culture predicated on supporting students who make mistakes is greater student willingness to seek help. Any student who fears expulsion won't risk admitting that they or their friends are using.

Data Collection

Healthy schools want to know the truth, including the fact that some of their students use and might be at risk. Even when the data are unflattering and troublesome, the truth is best. Effective prevention programs and policies require a clear understanding of the nature and scope of the problem. Schools should periodically gather information on student use through anonymous surveys administered by a third party. Evidence shows that, under such circumstances, students will respond honestly, and the information can be used to inform program development.

Prevention Programs

Armed with information about student use, attitudes about use, and beliefs about the level of use among peers, schools can design effective prevention programs. Use often begins during middle school, so schools should implement age-appropriate programs that begin in late elementary school and continue through high school.

Programs for younger students should focus on the impact good health has on academic performance and the negative effects of alcohol and drugs. As students advance, they should get specific information about the physiological impact of these substances. In high school, students should have these facts reinforced, but should also hear directly from speakers who have themselves suffered the consequences of using. Finding speakers is not difficult, because sharing stories is central to 12-step programs.

An especially promising prevention approach uses social norms data. Behaviors that are believed to be commonplace or "normal" are far more likely to occur. Even though alcohol and drug use among adolescents is widespread, research indicates that students exaggerate the extent of their peers' use. The belief that "everybody does it" normalizes the behavior and creates not-so-subtle pressure to conform. Conversely, when students find out that many of their peers use rarely or not at all, they're less likely to use themselves. Schools should gather this information and share it in compelling ways.

Many students have reported that they use in order to combat stress and boredom. Some of both are probably inevitable, but schools can adopt policies and programs that make a difference. Schools should adopt schedules that give students breaks during the day that provide opportunities for nutrition and relaxation. Similarly, schools should avoid the common practice of scheduling activities, review sessions, meetings, etc., during lunch, which should instead be a time when students eat and relax with their friends and teachers. Schools should limit the number of tests and/or papers due on a given day to no more than two. A simple test calendar strictly adhered to by faculty reduces student stress and fosters higher quality work.

Schools should also offer classes and activities that are known to reduce stress. Excellent examples are yoga and mindfulness training. Another promising innovation is peer leadership programs. They can take many forms, but typically involve carefully selected and trained older students (often seniors) working in a mentoring relationship with younger ones. The peer leaders should, in part, be selected for their willingness to model healthy attitudes about alcohol and drug use.

Schools should also offer opportunities for students to engage in healthy activities. Students frequently use alcohol and drugs on Friday nights to unwind from the week. An ideal alternative is for the school to host events that engage the students' creative talents. "Coffeehouse" events that include music, poetry readings, and stand-up comedy routines engage students with diverse interests.

Policy

No programs can ensure that all students will consistently maintain sobriety. Clear policies are essential to inform students of the school's behavioral expectations and the consequence for transgressions. No school would condone any level of student use of alcohol or drugs; but it is, nonetheless, vitally important to state this explicitly and to clarify the school's jurisdiction. Consequences for breaking school rules should be certain and progressive. A second or third offense should result in escalating discipline, up to expulsion, if it becomes clear that the student is unwilling to learn from mistakes. It's not enough simply to put the expectations in a handbook; rather, there should be regular reminders through various media and forums.

Enlisting Parents as Allies

Too often, parents look to the school not only to educate their children, but also to develop character and solve all manner of social problems. Opinions may vary as to the appropriateness of the school taking on roles that have traditionally been the purview of churches and parents, but it's clear that schools can be successful in these endeavors only when they work in partnership with parents. It is essential for parents to be familiar with the school's expectations and programs. As with students, it's not enough to articulate policies in a handbook. Rather, schools should offer forums for parents to learn about the effects of adolescent alcohol and drug use, the laws governing such use, and effective ways to detect and combat their child's possible experimentation. This sort of outreach to parents is successful only in a climate of trust and respect. When parents view the school as primarily concerned with the health and welfare of students, they are much more willing to embrace and support its rules.

Additionally, in a climate of trust, when Heads of Schools and Principals have good cause to suspect that a particular student is using alcohol or drugs, they can and should meet and discuss the issue with the parents. The discussion should be expressed as a concern, not an allegation, and there should not be a disciplinary outcome. Testing the student should be encouraged as a means of confirming or removing the concern, and the emphasis should remain on the student's welfare.

Counseling

Sadly, it's inevitable that some students will use. In schools that have built a culture of trust and willingness to help, they are much more likely to reach out to counselors, who should have training in detecting alcoholism and addiction, and be familiar with outside treatment resources. When possible, schools should have a confidential drug counselor on retainer, but not on staff. This added level of anonymity can encourage students to seek help.

Schools cannot prevent every student from experimenting with alcohol and drugs. But they can reduce the number of those who use and mitigate the self-destructive consequences. Success depends on consistent, sustained effort based on the conviction that student wellness is central to effective education. The effort is worth it.

About the Author

Michael Pratt, a distinguished educator, is a consultant with m/Oppenheim Associates, currently on assignment as Interim Head of School at St. John's Episcopal School in Orange County, CA. Prior to joining m/Oppenheim, Michael taught history at an independent school and a university in the Washington, D.C. area; served as a Program Officer at the National Endowment for the Humanities; was Academic Dean at Menlo School in Atherton, CA; and was Head of Brentwood School in Los Angeles, CA for a decade. He and his wife maintain their permanent residence in Napa, CA where Michael serves on the Napa County Advisory Board for Alcohol and Drug Programs and on the board of the Wolfe Center, which provides alcohol and drug prevention and treatment services to adolescents.

[i] See "Excessive Drinking Costs U.S. $223.5 Billion" on the Centers for Disease Control and Prevention website: www.cdc.gov/Features/Alcohol Consumption.

[ii] See "Addiction Medicine: Closing the Gap between Science and Practice," June 2012 on The National Center on Addiction and Substance Abuse. www.casacolumbia.org

[iii] See the findings reported in the 2012 Monitoring the Future survey. Monitoring the Future is a survey of alcohol and illicit drug use by 8th, 10th, and 12th grade students, administered annually by the University of Michigan's Institute for Social Research. The survey has been funded since its inception in 1975 by the National Institute on Drug Abuse.

Made in the USA
Middletown, DE
04 January 2015